D0709694

A WAKE DIGEST

This is a collection of twenty-four short papers, arranged in three groups, each commenting on particular facets of James Joyce's *Finnegans Wake*. Some of the papers have not been published before while others have been revised. The majority of papers are taken from *A Wake Newslitter*, a mimeographed (and later letterpress) journal published in Australia. The *Newslitter* allows Joycean scholars to contribute to general discussion of theories about Joyce and his *Wake* and to receive speedy printing of their articles.

Discussions in this book cover such diverse subjects as Joyce's use of forty languages, a theory on the possible reference to the Tetragrammaton in *Finnegans Wake*, music theory and its importance, socio-political parallels, anecdotes and comments on the Dublin theatres, and a problem in geometry.

A WAKE

carefully digesting the very wholesome criticism—163.36

DIGEST

edited by Clive Hart and Fritz Senn

SYDNEY UNIVERSITY PRESS
for Australian Humanities Research Council

SYDNEY UNIVERSITY PRESS

Press Building, University of Sydney

U.S.A. Pennsylvania State University Press
NEW ZEALAND   Price Milburn and Company Limited
ELSEWHERE   Methuen and Company Limited, London
and their agents

First published 1968

National Library of Australia registry number AUS 67-657

Printed at The Griffin Press, Adelaide
and registered in Australia for transmission by post as a book

CONTENTS

* Hitherto unpublished

ACKNOWLEDGMENTS

Quotations from *Finnegans Wake* are included by kind permission of Faber and Faber, Ltd, The Viking Press, Inc., and the Administrators of the James Joyce Estate.

We wish also to thank the following for the granting of copyright permissions: George Allen & Unwin, Ltd, for passages from Otto Jespersen's *An International Language*; Grove Press, Inc. and Dr Michael Hoffman, for a passage from Henry Miller's *Tropic of Cancer*; Methuen and Co., Ltd, for passages from S. A. O. Fitzpatrick's *Dublin: a Historical and Topographical Account of the City*.

EDITORIAL NOTE

A Wake Newslitter began publication in March 1962, having arisen out of conversations between Mr Senn and myself during the summer of 1961. We planned it as an informal journal in which studies of *Finnegans Wake* might be quickly and easily published, so that information about current Joycean studies could be made readily available to the scholarly fraternity. Its reading public rapidly increased in numbers so that by February 1964 the *Newslitter* was able to abandon its original mimeographed format and re-emerge in letterpress.

During 1962 and 1963 eighteen issues of the mimeographed *Newslitter* were published. The present volume is a selection of articles and notes which appeared during that period, together with a number of hitherto unpublished articles by contributors to the journal. Many of the reprinted articles have been revised for publication in this *Digest*, some of them extensively. It should be noted that one of the most significant articles ever to appear in the mimeo *Newslitter* has, however, been omitted: this is Thornton Wilder's 'Giordano Bruno's Last Meal in *Finnegans Wake*' (No. 6, October 1962, pp. 1-7), which has been reprinted, with some emendations, in *The Hudson Review*, vol. XVI, no. 1, Spring 1963, pp. 74-9.

University of Newcastle, N.S.W.   CLIVE HART
    November 1967

I   Source Studies and General Explication

The Elephant in the Belly: Exegesis
of *Finnegans Wake*

I shall lay my filing cards on the table from the outset: it seems to me that for many years the situation with respect to the explication of *FW* has been deteriorating, and that if current indications are to be believed the situation is likely to grow still worse before we see any improvement. The mass of inferior critical and exegetical material found its genesis in early and wildly speculative readings of the text which formed the basis of an in-bred school—if that is the right word—of Joycean studies, a school which has been established for so long that it hardly thinks of questioning its assumptions. But we must be careful in applying a corrective since this also is likely to have its dangers. I want, in this paper, to set out what seem to me to be the twin possibilities of extremism and to suggest a number of *points de repère* for future explication. I shall not attempt to develop a detailed theory of explication, but shall propose, instead, a limited number of simple working hypotheses and axioms.

FW has been a splendid encouragement to excess ever since the days of 'Work in Progress'. The colourful verbal revolutionaries of Jolas' transitional Paris have been succeeded by a less rebellious generation of critics and writers, but, although creative extremism has apparently had its day, critical standards still seem to undergo a strange shift of emphasis whenever people get a copy of *FW* into their hands. The book still represents to some readers—quite falsely, I believe—the high point of the die-hard literary movements of the early 30s, and there is still to be found a small band of critics who want to treat *FW* as they would the poems of Jolas and Hugo Ball, or the prose of Souppault and Eluard. Such criticism is so badly focused as to be negligible. Needing even less discussion are such matters as slovenly scholarship, inaccuracy of presentation, and garbling of facts. These things are to be met with in any branch of literary studies, and although they tend to be very frequent in published research on *FW*, and, perhaps because of the unfamiliar nature of the terrain and the difficulty of checking assertions, more dangerous in this field than in another, they are a general matter concerning all scholars and differ only in degree in this instance.

3

The really important issues are so simple that they often tend to be overlooked. They are all implied, in fact, in the intelligent layman's response to the explicator: 'How do you know that these things really are in the text? Did Joyce intend them? If not, on what grounds do you justify them?' The layman is in strictly comparable difficulties with, say, *Hamlet*, but in the case of *FW* he seems to be much more at sea because he can rely on no easily discoverable system of values and commonly possessed standards from which to begin the exploration of textual possibilities more remote than those which appear on the surface. The fact that Joyce does indeed make use of such common critical and aesthetic property beneath the surface of the book is of little help to the layman, since these common possessions are buried under a mass of particulars so forbidding that only the initiate (in the present state of Joyce studies) can extract them. And so we turn in gyrogyrorondo.

For the average reader—and all too often for the average student as well—the common standards have been replaced by a set of publicly announced critical views on *FW* which have been taken for granted as the best basis on which to work. The highly flavoured dicta of the *Skeleton Key* have very often been accepted without question, while categorical statements about Joyce's methods of word-formation and word-association have been reiterated for years without their being subjected to scrutiny by application to selected passages of text. One suspects, indeed, that a great many people have written about *FW* without devoting to it even as much time as they would to *Ulysses*. Many a false trail has been started, many a chimera hunted through the dense pages as a result. The danger is not so much that incorrect readings will be offered (ultimately there is, I think, no such thing as an incorrect reading of *FW*), as that we shall lose our sense of proportion in assessing the relative importance of readings. I shall return to that point at the end of the paper.

The alternative danger—hitherto less familiar—lies in too great an insistence on the primacy of Joyce's initial and particular intentions, with the consequent undervaluing of, first, Joyce's general theory of *FW* and, second, the book's indications of its own 'intentions' as distinct from those of its creator. While Joyce has clearly included words and word-parts with specific denotations, to ignore which would be to impoverish the sense of the text, there is nothing to suggest either that he wanted to hold the meaning of *FW* within these rigid limits, or that the book will appear less valuable if we allow our explications freer rein. Everyone is prepared, these days, to grant a certain measure of autonomy to poetry—*Dichtung*—and to allow sense and imagery to be to some extent self-controlling. The stumbling block with *FW* obtrudes because there we must take into account the further possibility that Joyce allows

4

some autonomy to word-formation, morphology, and semantics. This is an entirely unfamiliar literary procedure which arouses a great deal of rather emotional opposition in some quarters. It is, apparently, well enough for the meanings of images to be undefined by an author, but it is not yet allowable for the denotations of individual words to be similarly indefinite. Now, at this stage I must stress that I am not on my way towards a justification of *FW* as cloud-material on to which we readers may project whatever sense seems best suited to our psyches. Far from it; I should like, indeed, to place the emphasis on the side of conservatism and reason, but I think it is as foolish to deny the validities of meanings which Joyce never consciously created as to deny them in the case of *Hamlet*—and few people, I suppose, will claim that *Hamlet* may be allowed to mean only what Shakespeare probably thought it meant. These considerations may seem elementary to the point of banality, but the extraordinarily lanate thinking of so much that has been said about *FW* in recent years makes some such approach advisable.

It is, of course, impossible to know exactly what Joyce consciously put into *FW*. Certain things can be discovered by recourse to the MSS, to the letters, and to other biographical sources, but we must be careful not to adopt too naïve an attitude to what the MSS tell us. Joyce seems to have been aware that his MSS would be read by future generations, so that they may not be the unswept literary workshop which they at first seem to resemble. It is, nevertheless, undeniable that their survival makes possible a fairly accurate tracing of the history and development of *one* aspect of the book: the constituent parts. One may wonder how legitimate it is to turn to the MSS for help; one may have one's doubts about the relevance of readings which only they can present; and Joyce's own attitude to their importance for the reader of *FW* seems to have been ambiguous, to say the least. But if we are enquiring about Joyce's conscious artistry they are of undoubted value. (On the whole they are most useful in the case of the chapters written earliest, since these tend to go through many draft stages—from a simple exposition in relatively plain English, to the complexities of the final text. As he got well into *FW*, Joyce started to write more spontaneously in his polyhedral style; many highly complicated sentences appear to have been written down in their final form without prior commitment to paper.)

An example of the pursuit of Joyce's intentions, and of the secondary help which the MSS afford by way of verification, was given us in the lists of Swahili words which Mr P. Wolff sent to *A Wake Newslitter*, and which were subsequently modified and corrected by Mr Jack Dalton.[1]

---

[1] *A Wake Newslitter*, no. 8, December 1962, pp. 2-4; no. 12, April 1963, pp. 6-12.

Mr Wolff based his lists on his own knowledge of Swahili and on personal experience of Africa, while Mr Dalton relied on dictionaries, source-studies, and the text of *FW* itself. I am not now concerned with the matter of scholarly skill. Mr Dalton presented us with a model of accuracy and acumen in the pursuit of facts. What one may make of the facts themselves is of more importance. Mr Dalton has demonstrated that certain words may be seen functioning as Swahili in the completed text, while if verification should be needed, the MSS show to anyone with a suitably loaded microfilm-reader and half an hour to spare that a large number of Swahili words were added to the text of *FW* at the same time. People only casually versed in Joycean studies are often highly sceptical of the suggestion that such things as Swahili words *really* are in *FW*. One glance at the MSS will dispel any doubts that these words really are to be interpreted as Swahili—*at least in the initial stage of their addition to the text*. Whether they are to be so interpreted in the final version of the book is a more sophisticated question to which I shall return later.

By means which I shall not treat in detail here—such things as the recognition of quotations, misprints, special spellings, proper names—it is possible to retrieve at least the core of what Joyce *put into FW*. He himself helps the reader, as is now well known, by the introduction of clues to his sources and to his frames of reference. The danger—a very serious one, in my view—lies in thinking that if all these clues are discovered and followed up, the book will be elucidated. The relatively new tendency towards spareness and caution in interpretation and explication is very welcome; it will correct the extravagances of those who seem to keep their eyes on the ceiling rather than on the text; but it may lead in the end to a machine-like loss of sensitivity. Mr Wolff, for example, suggested that 'rima' (200.33) and 'tembo' (209.11) might mean 'pit for catching large animals', and 'elephant', respectively. In discussing these Mr Dalton says, first: 'I'm afraid I'll have to draw the line on there being an "elephant" in ALP's belly', and then hopes for a plethora of guffaws at the idea that Anna should be seen digging a Very Dip Pit for Heffalumps. These rejections show, I think, three things: first, rather too much insistence on a rational reading of the text; second, a certain lack of artistic sensibility; third, the unwarranted ignoring (in this instance, at any rate) of Joyce's use and abuse of the surrealist mode which was so popular during the heyday of the book's composition, and which he so richly parodies and cunningly pillages. I am not suggesting that the particular readings in question—elephants and pits—are necessarily of great aesthetic value, but I do suggest that they are by no means to be put aside merely on the grounds of their oddity, or because of their inconsistency with other levels of interpretation. We must not dismiss too lightly Joyce's delight in the chance meanings of words, the peculiar interaction often caused by their juxtaposition, and the power of verbal circumstance. That the accidents of language could stuff an elephant into Anna's world-bearing womb was the kind of thing that delighted Joyce —as his personal associates are unanimous in maintaining. Whether Joyce himself ever knew about the stuffing, in this particular instance, is quite beside the point. To dismiss such a reading as ridiculously incorrect is to ignore the better half of the book.

But let me move once more from the particular to the general. My principal objection to the logical and rational method of reading *FW* is that it may lead to the expulsion of poetry. I do not wish to equate poetry with disorder, but as soon as we start saying to ourselves that certain readings will not allow sentences to parse properly, we should ask whether we are not trying to turn *FW* into a prose palimpsest, each level of which can be stated in normal grammatical English. This is a grave literary sin. It seems evident that many readings of *FW* which are wholly acceptable will not 'make sense' in any ordinary way. As I have already pointed out, it is certainly possible, by means of a reversal of Joyce's process of composition, rationally to extract and isolate the deposits of discrete pieces of denotation from which the book was originally compounded. I am not suggesting that this pursuit will lead to a denial of the interrelationships of constituent parts, nor that its exponents claim the whole to be no more than the sum of the parts. What I am suggesting, however, is that it constitutes a most restrictive form of fallacious intentionalism.

Now, I am well aware that the Intentional Fallacy can be, and too often has been, invoked to support over-personalized theories of the significance of works of art and, as I said, I do not hold that *FW* means just what each reader may want it to mean. But I do believe that Joyce's usual approach to his art supports the suggestion that he allowed his works at least some referential autonomy (which does not, of course, mean complete autonomy). I do not, therefore, wish to dismiss the importance of Joyce's intentions; in subsequent pages I shall frequently refer to them. Since, however, an anti-intentionalist reading of the text seems, paradoxically, to have Joyce's sanction—to have been, as it were, part of his intention—my occasional appeals to Joyce's practice and attitudes will be in support of both a closer examination of what he put into *FW* and a willingness on the part of the explicator to allow the relevance of readings beyond what Joyce consciously set out to achieve.

Although I agree that the first and most important thing to do in explicating *FW* is to deal with the material included by intention, it may not be so ridiculous as one at first imagines to allow the validity even of readings which Joyce never had *any possibility* of including. He seems to have wanted meanings to accrete in his text by hindsight as well as by means of his own constant redistortions of the vocabulary. Both referent and reference were for Joyce autonomous and in a state of flux, their interrelationships constantly changing. This is a process which Joyce saw as continuous and endless. How else are we to interpret his delight in the Finns and the Russian Generals? Is not, by his own admission, the Finno-Russian conflict of the Second World War a minor theme in *FW*? Joyce wanted to be a prophet; the meaning of his book projects forwards as well as backwards, as the text repeatedly insists. This kind of thing can obviously and very easily be taken too far. But it may serve to emphasize that, in respect to details of the text, intent at the time of writing is not the only consideration.

The Dedalian withdrawal can also be exaggerated, of course. Joyce was by no means as detached as he often liked to pretend, and I believe the available biographical evidence shows him to have been much simpler, more committed, more bourgeois in his attitude to literature, than Mr Kenner, in particular, has depicted him. In the past we have read rather too much about manicuro-mania. And yet there always remains some truth in the image of the uninvolved Artist-God. I take a mid-position, then, and claim for *FW* no more than I claim for any poetry: that is to say, that it often means more than Joyce meant it to mean (just as it sometimes means less); that it is likely often to mean slightly different things to author and reader, and that this disparity is of no significance unless an artistically debilitating ambiguity results.

I should like now to set out in summary form my own present approach to this literary phenomenon. I think that Mr Atherton's view of *FW* as a cosmos governed by its own laws has been demonstrated beyond the need for further comment. It is from this position that I start. The concept of correctness must, I believe, give way entirely to pragmatism. A reading is to be accepted if it provides answers. But we must take care: by this method it is possible to prove literally anything. Take any passage at random and you can demonstrate that it is about, say, the twenty-four golden umbrellas of the King of Thailand. The method is, of course, applicable to any work of literature. Mr Dalton has suggested to me that the opening scene of *Hamlet* can be shown to be entirely concerned with sexual intercourse. The principle therefore seems to be a lunatic one, and yet I believe that in the case of *FW* it has a certain validity. Anything in *FW* is indeed about anything else—*but only in the last of an infinite regress of planes of meaning*. The all-important question, in my view, is how to get these planes of meaning into the right order, and into the right perspective. I have no doubt, myself, that all the planes are there.[2] But there is no point in assuming the book to be a meaningless jumble, which is the way it seems if we do not keep the frames of reference separated. To continue the analogy with the physical world: in the last plane everything is like everything else—a cricket cap is discovered to be identical with a cracked cup when the universe is an undifferentiated agglomeration of energy; in less remote planes various coherent configurations of world-material are stabilized and made apprehendable by the functioning of a variety of laws. In both the physical universe and *FW* chaos results if we do not distinguish between the laws of physics, say, and the laws of society, or between the world-views of scientist and mystic. I would ask the reader to remember the cricket cap and the cracked cup. That is genuine surrealism, producing a witty high-lighting of welded disparates. But it also leads towards a loss of identity. There is a point beyond which the flux ceases to be interesting.

There is a danger that the cultivation of one plane will lead to the exclusion of others of comparable importance. I think that some of the ambiguities and contradictions in Joyce's own statements about *FW* arise because he allows such a multiplicity of planes of meaning. Thus, he might tell one reader that a certain passage depends upon this or that particular piece of information, and tell another that specific allusions may be ignored. The letter to Frank Budgen about the Eastern and Western Churches is an example of the first,[3] while the famous statement to Professor Straumann exemplifies the second approach:

> One should not pay any particular attention to the allusions to place-names, historical events, literary happenings and personalities, but let the linguistic phenomenon affect one as such.[4]

There is a level, then, at which the Swahili words in ALP are probably not to be interpreted as Swahili at all—and I am not sure whether I think it more important to read them as Swahili or not. A lot of specific meanings emerge if we do so read them, but perhaps there is an even more valuable level at which the primarily decorative nature of the Swahili references is overlaid by senses not dependent on this linguistic knowledge. I do not yet know where I stand on this issue—the factors involved are

---

[2] *See* such statements in *FW* as that at 109.27: ' . . . capable of being stretched, filled out, if need or wish were . . . '. And readers who doubt whether anything in *FW* can represent the author's own views might look at the letter to Frank Budgen dated 20 August 1939 (*Letters*, I, p. 406).

[3] *See* F. Budgen, *James Joyce and the Making of Ulysses*. Bloomington, 1960, pp. 315-6.

[4] H. Straumann, 'Last Meeting with Joyce', in *A James Joyce Yearbook*, ed. M. Jolas. Paris 1949, p. 114.

very complex—and I shall say only that I suspect, for example, that the English words 'wend' and 'wander' are *much* more important to an understanding of ALP than is our knowledge that 'Wendawanda' (199.12) contains a Swahili word meaning virtually the same thing as the English word that follows it.[5] (I am not suggesting, of course, that 'Wendawanda' means *only* 'wend' and 'wander', nor that Mr Dalton thinks it means only 'a fingerthick'. I am concerned here only with a priority for these two partial readings.) We must remember that, for all its pedantries, *FW* is a work of imaginative literature, and that imagination ought always to have the ascendancy over scholarship.

For whom, in any case, was Joyce writing *FW*? For a variety of audiences, no doubt, from the most erudite to the most naïve. Joyce's comments in his letters and in conversation make it quite clear that he had the common reader in mind as much as the literary sophisticate. He intended the book to contain something for everybody, hoped that readers from any part of the world would find rivers they could recognize, dialects with which they were familiar. He said that he was writing in a 'Big Language'. This is not to deny the value of the purely scholarly approach to *FW*, which can be made as relevant and as valuable as the scholarly approach to Shakespeare. But there seems every reason to approve of Mr Wolff's approach as well as of Mr Dalton's. Part of Joyce's aim, with his Big Language, was evidently to provide a level of significance to readers familiar with Swahili as living speech. To ignore the somewhat imprecise possibilities of meaning which thus arise, and to insist on 'correctness' of interpretation as given by the source-dictionaries, is the more scholarly procedure, but it is also rather over-solemn. Without an appeal to the source-books, living experience will often lead the reader to interpretations at variance with Joyce's original specific intentions, as Mr Wolff's example shows. The consistency of the text is not alone sufficient to define the limits of those intentions. The text must first be used to lead to the sources (as it usually does, in the long run) and these in their turn examined to find the limits. This point seems to me to be of very great importance. Did Joyce expect his readers to root out the sources? In many cases, as recently published source-studies have shown, he does in fact encourage the scholar in these pursuits. But the scholar is only one among many classes of readers of *FW*. In so far as the Swahili in *FW* is there to be interpreted as Swahili, Joyce puts it into the book so that *those familiar with the language* will recognize it. The more his readers know, the more they will see (and also, as a corollary, the more doubtful readings they will reject). The limits of recognition are blurred,

[5] *See*, however, Mr Halper's excellent discussion of linguistic counterpoint, pp. 54-5.

and I am not sure that Joyce would consider the originally intended meanings, or even the consistency of the text (as demonstrated by scholarly research) to be any more 'correct' than the spontaneous and sometimes 'inaccurate' readings of a Mr Wolff. The limits of scholarly and spontaneous recognition are not necessarily identical, and I see no reason to suppose that they should be. Consistency of the text is a comparatively new shibboleth which arose out of the rejection of intentionalism. It needs critical scrutiny, and may prove to be yet another Grand Fallacy.

The scholarly approach, which attempts to clarify and define with precision (and to which, I must add, I am myself ultimately committed) is a highly artificial way of reading *FW*. We are bringing literary experience to bear on it, rather than personal experience, and I have no doubt which of the two Joyce would prefer to see used. Of course, if we are to get beyond the limits of our personal experience, the richness of the text forces us into scholarship. But, having engaged in our literary researches, we must try to let our recondite bits of information develop in our imaginations into something more vital than facts if our reading of *FW* is to be of relevance to human beings. In case I may seem to imply the contrary, I shall add that I know that Mr Dalton recognizes this truth very well. Too many attempts to explicate *FW* fail, however, to progress beyond the facts.

Use of the imagination is in any case essential to an adequate perception of Joyce's planes of meaning. How far may we go in exercising it to discover new planes? I think that temperament probably determines the extent to which we spontaneously see relationships between words and images. To Mr Dalton's question: 'does anyone honestly think ... that "sufuria" or "susurika" ... come close to "susuria"?'[6] I answer, for myself, emphatically, 'Yes, very close.' As to his further question concerning 'umvolosy' and 'fuliza' I answer 'No.' Again, though 'mbwa' is not, as Mr Dalton rightly says, 'umbas', the latter word certainly suggests the former to me; and, furthermore, I am sure that it would do so to Joyce himself. (There are many examples in *FW* of suggestions much more remote than this—examples which can be demonstrated beyond any doubt, if need be, by recourse to the mss.) Whether Joyce *intended* these suggestions is, of course, not in question at this point.

As I suggested above, I believe that Joyce's general attitudes to *FW* are more important than his particular notions about individual words, over which he does not exercise complete control. Ultimately, however, and perhaps more plainly than with any other work of literature, it is

---

[6] *A Wake Newslitter*, no. 12, April 1963, p. 10.

the direct relationship between the book and the reader which determines the value of an explication, the 'truth' of a meaning. The truths enunciated by the scholars are no more, and no less, absolute than those enunciated, about the physical universe, by the scientists. My fears concerning the undesirable results which may possibly follow from too scholarly an approach to the text give way, however, to increasing dismay at the incoherencies of the opposite approach. I come down heavily on the side of the rationalists, at least for the time being, because I think that little progress of any value can be made in the more remote planes of significance until the nature of Joyce's central intentions is more fully documented. I shall conclude, then, with a few propositions about the reading of the book:

1: Every syllable is meaningful. *FW* contains no nonsense, and very little onomatopoeia, etc. Joyce deals principally in semantemes.

2: An explication is lacking unless it accounts for every syllable and justifies every letter.

3: Elements in an explication which are of widely disparate natures must—unless they can be seen to have hidden relationships—fit into a number of different but coherent planes of meaning.

4: If an element of explication does not fit into such a coherent plane it is probably irrelevant except on that last plane where meaning dissolves because everything corresponds to everything else.

5: The most important task of the explicator is to sort out the planes of meaning into an order of precedence.

6: *FW* is, throughout, a work of imagination and should not be read as a biographical or factual record of any sort, except in so far as James Joyce is a part of the world it describes.

Clive Hart

Music Lesson

Among the broadest divisions of *FW* III.4 (555-590) are the four sections, of radically varied lengths, belonging to the old men. These sections are signalled by carefully paralleled passages:

> Side point of view. First position of harmony. Say! Eh? Ha! . . . Matt. Male partly masking female. (559.21-22)

> Jeminy, what is the view which now takes up a second position of discordance, tell it please? Mark! You notice it in that rereway because the male entail partially eclipses the femecovert. It is so called for its discord the meseedo. (564.1-4)

> Third position of concord! Luk! Excellent view from front. Sidome. Female imperfectly masking male. (582.29-31)

> Fourth position of solution. How johnny! Finest view from horizon. . . . Two me see. Male and female unmask we hem. (590.22-24)

The purpose of this paper is to clarify one aspect of the parallelism.

The reader is first obliged to learn by rote these facts:

1: In solmization there are two systems, called movable-do and fixed-do. In the movable-do system, do is the 1st tone, mi the 3rd, si the 7th. (The syllable si, standard in Europe, is equivalent to the ti now generally taught in America.)
  In the fixed-do system, C = do, E = mi, B = si.
  There is one major key of the twelve in which the movable-do and fixed-do systems become identical, the key of C.

2: In German terminology the note B is called H. Therefore, si = H (fixed-do, or movable-do in C major).

3: In the German alphabet, and therefore in German musical terminology, C is pronounced "tsay," E is pronounced "eh" (when pronounced to rhyme with "say"), and H is pronounced "ha."

Now, applying this information, we have:

Say! Eh? Ha!
C   E   H

meseedo

E H C

Sidome

H C E

Two me see

C   E   H

In a word, our "Favourite Hero."[1]

The letters HCE can be arranged in six ways. Joyce chose a method which gave him the desired four. This method is best described as shifting the first letter to the end. (It is cumbersome, as well as backwards, to think of it as putting the last two letters first.)
Therefore:

CEH

EHC

HCE

CEH

This means that the chapter is circular, since the last arrangement is identical with the first. ("Fourth position of solution.") It should be noted that this method allowed Joyce to begin and end with the letters in ascending order, alphabetically and musically.

Furthermore, if the repetition is omitted and the letters printed in a square

C E H

E H C

H C E,

an hermetic symmetry is discovered. In this square the three arrangements of letters appear twice each, at right angles:

C E H   E   H

E   E H C   C

H   C   H C E[2]

---

[1] Those wishing to see him foot the staff can refer to *WN* 16, Sept. 1963, p. 2.

Emendation of "Favorite" (306.21): In the first draft (B. M. Add. MS 47478.152b) and in the fair copy from which the typescript was made (-.176) Joyce wrote "Favourite." The typist's "Favorite" (-.203) persisted into *FW*. A similar instance provided by the St Kevin episode is instructive: On 47488.67 the "centre" of preceding drafts was typed "center." (That page of typescript is particularly corrupt; see my "Hardest Crux" in *JJQ* 3, Spring 1964.) This "center" persisted through the two succeeding typescripts, through the galleys, and into the (missing) page proofs. Joyce's correction is found on -.238: 'Page 606 line 3 from top instead of "center" read "centre".' (Cf. the essay title "*My Favourite Hero*" in *U*, 685.21.)

[2] Read in exact reverse, of course, the square yields the other three arrangements of HCE, each one twice, at right angles.

A peculiarity of the passages is that the descriptions "harmony," "discordance," "concord," and "solution" do not refer to the music itself, though the words are, of course, used in musical terminology. For example, the second sequence—EHC—is a resolution and concordant, yet it is called discordant. Perhaps I am missing something. More likely, however, it is merely that when a number of things are being done at once it is rare for each level to fit at every other level. Thus, the "fourth position" is not one of *musical* "solution," but is a resolution of the chapter.

It is possible, though, that the music is meant to be meaningful on certain levels. For example, in the first and last arrangements the sequence ends on the 7th, the leading tone. This tone is that of least rest in the scale; it yearns irresistibly towards the tonic, the 1st tone. In the first case this dynamic can be thought of as propelling into the chapter, and in the second it can be thought of as propelling into Book IV. Thus in the "fourth position" there is a contrast between momentary calm and beauty and the strong forward propulsion of the leading tone, this latter also finding expression in 590.24 ff. Tenuous, but not improbable, I think. Joyce may well have attached such significances to the music resulting from his HCE-square.

Though it is not in the least necessary to "prove" what is quite beyond the question of proof (as correct *FW* explications, correctly presented, always are or tend to be), manuscript evidence is invariably of interest and value. In the left margin of B. M. Add. MS 47482A.30b, beside what is now *FW* 559.20, Joyce wrote:

```
H C E     C E H
sidomy    E H C
          H C E
```

Except that it lacks a repetition of CEH, the list is exactly as used. The square is identical with that given above. It will be noted that the syllables of "sidomy" begin precisely beneath their respective letters.

If the chronology given in Mr Hayman's "Draft Catalogue" is correct (and I have no evidence to contradict him in this matter), Joyce wrote in substantially its present form what now stands as the third section (as well as parts of the second) some time before hitting on the four-part division, and, *inter alia*, the musical HCEs. At least he did not yet know where the sections began and ended. But in the first draft of *FW* 559.20 ff. he wrote "First position," and then began to add other features of the parallel openings. A false start in sol-fa was made with "Domicy." This is CEH, as now, but did not survive the draft. By later adding

"Say! Eh? Ha!" Joyce established the key of C major, thus merging the movable-do and fixed-do systems.[3]

Why these sol-fa HCEs, beyond their ornamental value? In this chapter the family is seen as a group, but "bad bold faathern," as in life, is dominant. In the openings of the first two sections the male partially hides the female. In the third we find "Female imperfectly masking male," yet the command is "show pon him now, will you! . . . Hokoway, in his hiphigh bearserk!" In the fourth they are equally seen—almost! Ambiguity is introduced by "hem," obsolete for both "them" and "him." The use of his initials in these important parallel passages, I think then, only emphasizes, for the millionth time, the vast importance of this "imposing everybody" so likeable and all too human.

Jack P. Dalton

[3] Paradoxically, perhaps the least of several considerations in his mind. It is quite possible that Joyce was Continental to the extent of thinking in terms of fixed-do (though living in France did not persuade him to exchange his euphonious do for ut), and therefore expected his readers to think likewise. I say this because of "musical me" at 124.25: "musical me" is "mi," and to find the sense the reader must read "E," which is to say, accept it as fixed-do.

And why "E"? I have lately been accused of complicity in the *Second Census*, whereas I have always maintained that when ready I would let it be known. Now is a time good enough, and I herewith follow my four HCEs with four Shems, one of them a Shemus: 124.17,21,24 ff.,27. Item 3 is the Shemus:

S as in shamrock ("grown in waterunspillfull Pratiland only," "Pratiland" being praty-land;
    this phrase originally read "grown in Ireland only")
H as in hen ("a playful fowl")
E as in fixed-do mi ("musical me")
M = "not you" (I don't know why. Joyce glossed the phrase with "U," which must
    indicate the path to be followed. See B.M. Add. MS 47482B.117 and -.122b for his notes,
    and -.116b for the draft of the passage.)
$\frac{U}{S}$ = "in any case" ("-us" being a case ending)

This is the "two and two" which "thinkers all put . . . together," the cause of the "sigh for shame" (so originally) which "separated modest mouths." It being grasped, "shamelessly," "shamrock," and "shyme" come to life, and we are in the way of becoming properly prepared for 125.23, the rousingly clear identification of our adumbrated letterwriter. "Small need after that . . . for quizzing. . . . " (!)

Especially in light of the manuscript evidence, it seems to me beyond doubt that the passage arose from "shamrock" and "Dame Partlet on her dungheap" immediately preceding. In the completed text these serve as a running start into the puzzle.

Emendation of "waterungspillfull" (124.24-25): The words "waterunspillfull Pratiland" were substituted for "Ireland" on 47473.100b. They were written one above the other in a narrow margin, and consequently the "P" of "Pratiland" runs into the "w" above and the rise of the "d" runs through the "s." The *transition* printer set "waterungspillfull Fratiland" (-.112), using the "s" twice, once as a "g" whose tail was supplied by the "d" below. Joyce caught only the "F." (The "waterunspillfull" of -.100b is run through or into at six other points, several vital, so that letters 3 and 4 are not absolutely certain, and the 5th extremely puzzling, being completely run through by the top of the "l" below and the complex having several strokes which I cannot account for on any grounds. Furthermore, letter 6 could conceivably be an "n." I cannot explicate the word with any combination of letters, but we can be sure the "g" is wrong, and this brings us closer to understanding.)

*re'*furloined notepaper (419.29)

For some time a 'purloined letter' has been lying in full view on the table of Mr Joyce's library. This is *A Classical Dictionary of the Vulgar Tongue* by Captain Francis Grose, published in London by S. Hooper in 1785. (Perhaps mentioned as 'Alderman Hooper', *Ulysses* 692.12?) In his monograph *The Personal Library of James Joyce*, Buffalo, 1955, Professor Thomas E. Connolly mentions this as one of the books in Joyce's possession. Below is a list of words apparently culled by Joyce from this dictionary. Some of the words below were, of course, in current use in the Dublin of Joyce's day and are found in the dictionary by coincidence.

A great many of the words in this list were contributed by Adaline Glasheen, a very gracious and generous lady who is prodigal with her recognition of the aid of others in her own work but who seems willing to help aspiring Joyceans without thought of credit.

Abram naked 26.19-20, 531.10, 546.17, 624.14
Act of Parliament a military term for small beer, five pints of which by an act of parliament a landlord was formerly obliged to give to each soldier gratis 392.35-6
All Nations a composition of all the different spirits sold in a dram shop collected in a vessel, into which the drainings of the bottles and quartern pots are emptied 11.20
Altitudes a man in his altitudes is drunk 4.33
Anthony Pig favourite or smallest pig in a litter 86.13-14
Armour pot valiant 23.08, 361.14
Aunt a bawd or procuress 314.24, 435.01
Bar Wig a wig between a dalmohay and a double cauliflower or full bottom 164.29, 559.25
Beard Splitter a man much given to wenching 229.20
Beggar's Bullets stones 79.31
Best to the best in Christendom; i.e. to the best **** in Christendom, a health formerly much in vogue 8.20
Black A**e a copperpot or kettle; pot calls kettle black a**e 251.11 (*see* 'stockpot', 251.05)

17

Bloss wife of a bully or shoplifter   237.12, 479.17, 528.05

Blue Ruin gin   39.34

Bull Beggar someone who scares children   82.05, 135.13

Caterpillar soldier   63.29

College any prison   385.08, 388.35

Colt's Tooth an old fellow who marries or keeps a young girl has a colt's tooth   534.08

Commons, House of privy   261.F2, 380.07

Cool Crape a shroud   9.31-2

Cundum the dried gut of a sheep worn by men in the act of coition. These machines were long prepared and sold by a matron of the name of Philips at the Green Cannister [9.32] in Half Moon Street   59.01, 375.12, 506.03

Dace twopence   201.14

Dangle to hang; to follow a woman without asking the question   534.36

Doodle a child's penis   299.F4, 306.08, 332.07, 337.29, 421.33, 464.22

Duchess a woman enjoyed with her pattens on is said to be made a duchess   171.25-6, etc.

Famms hands   251.12   possibly a double pun in the sense of handsome   420.10

Fat as a Hen in the Forehead said of meagre persons   275.13

Fieri Facias a red-faced man is said to be served with a writ of *fieri facias*   196.33, 279.F08, 279.F15

Flash of Lightning glass of gin   426.29 *and* 30

Fubsy plump   (*Ulysses* 41.21, 557.05)

Glim a candle   379.23, 585.05

Gluepot a parson; from joining men and women in matrimony   329.08   (*Ulysses* 418.10 *and* 11)

Grogham a horse   399.09

Impure whore   24.24, 234.30

Jark a seal   558.17

Jock to enjoy a woman   7.35, 33.28, 511.36, 575.26

Ladybirds lewd women   416.12, 534.36

Latitat an attorney   50.17

Lib lie together   250.19, 302.23

Lobscouse a dish much eaten at sea composed of salt beef, biscuit and onions well peppered and stewed together   467.17

Madge private parts of a woman   420.07, 459.04

Merkin counterfeit hair for the monosyllable   364.28, 387.28

Mettle the semen   313.27, 359.04, 604.36

Mine Uncle pawnbroker   101.09

Miss Laycock monosyllable   279.F02

Miss Molly an effeminate fellow   360.28

Mizzle elope, run off   468.26, 523.29

Morning Drop gallows   210.28

Mort a woman or wench   511.33 (*Ulysses* 418.26)

Mulligrubs low spirits   245.26, 321.33

Nap to cheat at dice; also to catch VD   9.06

Pluck a Rose what a woman says when going to necessary house which
   in country stands in garden   21.15, 22.03

Plugtail penis   10.13 ('tailoscrupp')

Prig thief   89.15, 173.08, 279.F17, 563.26

Prigging lying with a woman   163.10

Proud desirous of copulation   248.05

Quim monosyllable   283.04 (*Ulysses* 560.41)

Red Shank a duck   411.33

Reverence excrement   249.32, 334.17, 511.01

Ribbons reins   250.04

Roger to bull or lie with a woman   554.03

Romeville London   6.04 (*Ulysses* 48.09, 188.35)

Salt lecherous   201.14

Scotch Greys lice   8.23

Shot poxed   192.02-3 with 'gunorrhal'

Silent Flute penis   43.32, 200.35, 343.36

Sooterkin a joke upon the Dutch women, supposing that by the constant
   use of stoves, that they place under their petticoats, they breed a
   kind of small animal in their bodies of the size of a mouse; when
   mature it slips out   311.23

Spice Island privy, fundament   263.F2, 456.20

Staggering Bob a calf just dropped and just able to stand, killed for veal
   in Scotland   (*Ulysses* 412.42, 413.07-09, 537.01-03)

Stargazer a horse who throws up his head; also a hedge whore   143.26,
   471.09

Stark Naked gin   264.F1

Strapping lying with a woman   396.07, 510.07

Sugar Stick the male organ   424.28, 485.08 (*Ulysses* 149.01)

Swaddlers Irish name for Methodists   (*Ulysses* 331.23)

Touch copulate   233.10

Wagtail whore   262.L4, 301.15, 377.14, 582.11

Welsh Comb fingers   (*Ulysses* 125.09)

Whirligigs testicles   27.20, 119.14-15

Wrinkle Bellied Whore one who has had a number of bastards; child-
   bearing leaves wrinkles in a woman's belly   321.15

NOTE: In case Captain Grose's inconsistent modesty cause confusion, it may be mentioned that the word 'monosyllable' always refers to the female organ ('monosyllable': 190.35, 306.26, 338.25).

Philip L. Graham

The Earwickers of Sidlesham

Now ... concerning the genesis of Harold or Humphrey Chimpden's
occupational agnomen ... and discarding once for all those theories
from older sources which would link him back with such pivotal ancestors
as ... the Earwickers of Sidlesham in the Hundred of Manhood ...
(30.01)

In February of 1962, in response to some tentative enquiries that I had
made concerning the history of her family, Miss Gertrude Earwicker of
Sidlesham in the Hundred of Manhood, Sussex, sent me the following
letter. With the exception of some omissions of personal matter it is
reproduced verbatim:

William Earwicker is the first one that we have known of coming to live
in Sidlesham, some time in the 17 century, he died there in 1793, as a
headstone in the Churchyard shows. His sons were William, John, &
George, John being our grandfather, he passed on before we were born,
so we did not know him. Our father Charles William used to tell us of
their school days etc, he died in 1922. Our grandfather (John) bought a
small farm, and built a house in 1858 Redgate Farm, the one that we sold
in September, our father, and us were all born there, I had no other home,
but as we are getting to our seventies, we could not carry on, and our
brother Arthur has no children to carry on either. Our great uncle had
a little school for the boys of Sidlesham at his cottage, he had been in the
Army, in the 52nd Foot Regiment, educated himself in his travels, I
believe taught them quite well in reading, writing, and arithematic, there
was not a school here then, afterwards they walked daily to Chichester,
(five miles) to finish their education, our father, and his brother Thomas,
and John were among the boys. Our grandfather (John) used to sound
the note on the pipe for the singing in the Church, (no organ) We
were told that he was accidentally shut in the Church on night, he had
gone into the belfry to look for an owl that was lodging there. Not
knowing how to get out he rang the bells furiously, which soon brought
someone to his rescue ... Earwickers now in Sidlesham, are myself
Gertrude my Sister Nellie Law, (widow) and my brother Arthur
Earwicker.

Miss Earwicker was kind enough to enclose a photograph of Redgate Farmhouse. It is a compact two-storey building, with centrally placed front door, casement windows on each side, and a row of three casement windows on the first floor. The house is set back a few yards from the road.

The story of John Earwicker's ringing the church bells may have something to do with the chimes which repeatedly ring out from the speckled church in *FW*. Miss Earwicker's slightly literary account of the story (N.B. the sentence beginning 'Not knowing how to get out . . . ') suggests that it has often been told in Sidlesham. It may very well have come to Joyce's notice.

'Manhood' is the name of the extreme south-west 'Hundred' (county division) of Sussex. Sidlesham is, as Joyce tells us, in Manhood Hundred. I visited Sidlesham in the summer of 1961. It is a rather sprawling, unattractive village, with little to interest the casual visitor. In mid-1923, when he was enthusiastically beginning *FW*, Joyce was staying for a time at Bognor (Ellmann, pp. 564 ff.) which is only a very few miles from Sidlesham. It was at this time that Joyce drafted I.2, which begins with the passage quoted above. It would seem likely that Joyce visited Sidlesham during his holiday in Sussex, and if so he may have learned of the Earwickers by seeing the many family headstones in the churchyard. These are almost all unremarkable, bearing inscriptions like the following (for George Earwicker):

> *Not gone from memory*
> *Not gone from love*
> *Gone to our Father's home above.*

A John and a James Earwicker are to be found, buried side by side.

The old, correct, pronunciation of the name is 'Erricker'—hence Joyce's use of variant names like 'Herrick or Eric' (30.09).

Clive Hart

Dublin Theatres

One of Joyce's source-books was undoubtedly *Dublin: A Historical and Topographical Account of the City*, by Samuel A. Ossory Fitzpatrick, (London, Methuen, 1907). The author's name appears at 133.27. The following references are all taken from Chapter VIII, on 'Dublin Theatres'.

On p. 249 we read about Thomas Sheridan, actor and manager of the Smock Alley Theatre (*see* 184.24, *and Census*):

> A tragic occurrence marked one of his performances of *Othello*. The part of Iago was taken by an actor named Layfield. When he came to the lines:
>
> > Oh, my Lord! beware of jealousy;
> > It is a green-eyed monster,
>
> he gave the latter as 'It is a green-eyed lobster.' He was at that moment struck with incurable madness, and died somewhat in the manner of Nat Lee the tragic poet.

This fatal slip is carried over into *FW*: 'But if this could see with its backsight he'd be the grand old greeneyed lobster' (249.02). It is repeated at 88.13: 'Certified? ... And how did the greeneyed mister arrive at the B.A.?'

In the eighteenth century, after 1760, there was a craze for opera in Dublin. Certain arias were immensely popular, among them 'Water Parted'. This aria (from Arne's *Artaxerxes*) was associated in particular with the Italian singer Tenducci. Both he and the song were ridiculed by the Dublin *gamins* in a street song:

> *Tenducci was a Piper's son,*
> *And he was in love when he was young,*
> *And all the tunes that he could play*
> *Was 'Water parted from the say !'*
>
> (Fitzpatrick, p. 253)

Joyce gives the old nursery rime about Tom the piper's son yet another twist by making it: 'Dour douchy was a sieguldson. He cooed that loud nor he was young. He cud bad caw nor he was gray Like wather parted

23

from the say.' (371.06). As the *Census* points out, both Tenducci and the song recur at 541.32.

On p. 255 Fitzpatrick quotes an announcement concerning the re-opening of Smock Alley Theatre on 5 November 1738:

> Whereas complaints have been made of the Plays being done too late, this is to give Notice that they intend to remedy this Inconvenience, to begin precisely at 6 o'clock, therefore 'tis hop'd all Gentlemen, Ladies & others who intend to favour them with their company will not exceed that hour.

This may have contributed something to the opening of Book II: 'Every evening at lighting up o'clock sharp and until further notice in Feenichts Playhouse.' At the end of Book I the time is 6 p.m. (213.18). Fitzpatrick goes on to mention the prices of Dublin theatres. Cf. 'Entrancings: gads, a scrab; the quality, one large shilling' (219.03).

Joyce may also have found a touch he needed in what Fitzpatrick calls 'the versatility of the Dublin stock companies' (pp. 256-7):

> At Crow Street Digges [*FW* 313.26] was playing 'Hamlet' and ruptured a blood-vessel. The play was immediately stopped and 'She Stoops to Conquer' substituted for it. The manager's apologies having been accepted, the performers, who were all in the house, hastily dressed and went on. A gentleman in the pit had left the building immediately before the accident to Digges, for the purpose of buying oranges. He was delayed for some little time, and having left 'Hamlet' in conversation with the 'Ghost,' found on his return the stage occupied by 'Tony Lumpkin' and his companions at the Three Jolly Pigeons. He at first thought he had mistaken the theatre, but an explanation showed him the real state of affairs.

In *FW* all actors play multiple parts, often simultaneously, and we all think, again and again, that we have mistaken the theatre. In particular, Joyce used the incident in the paragraph beginning 323.25, where *She Stoops* and *Hamlet* are among the things that go on at the same time. Tony Lumpkin appears as 'tummelumpsk' and 'Toni Lampi', while Hamlet and the ghost are implied in 'ghustorily spoeking, gen and gang, dane and dare, like the dud spuk of his first foetotype' (323.35). Ibsen's *Ghosts* (*Gengangere*) are also present. In 'their saussyskins, the lumpenpack' (324.12) the set has been changed back to that of *She Stoops*: 'change all that whole set' (324.14).

The same sort of interfusion of tragic and comic, which is of course a constant feature of *FW*, is to be found in another incident which occurred at the Theatre Royal in the nineteenth century:

During Bunn's management a stage-struck amateur named Luke Plunkett, member of a respectable family resident near Portmarnock, appeared as 'Richard III.' Some of his readings of well-known passages were exceedingly erratic, and his death scene so amused the audience that they insisted on its repetition, with which demand the tragedian solemnly complied. (pp. 264-5)

This delightful incident appears in one of HCE's epithets: 'when Dook Hookbackcrook upsits his ass booseworthies jeer and junket but they boos him oos and baas his aas when he lukes like Hunkett Plunkett' (127.17). The worthies boosing in Earwicker's pub, Richard III's enemies triumphing at Bosworth Field, and an amused Dublin audience laughing and booing and asking Luke Plunkett to repeat his performance (as everything in *FW* is repeated) form close and fitting parallels. In an exceedingly erratic reading of the well-known opening of the play— 'Now eats the vintner over these contents oft with his sad slow munch for backonham' (318.20)—Richard is surrounded by food. The abundance of food in the passage at 127.17 suggests that the bodies of the fallen victims serve as food for a totemistic-Eucharistic meal. The 'booseworthies' who 'boos . . . oos' their victims are, of course, no better than their defeated enemies, as is suggested by overtones of the German and Dutch words for evil. Furthermore, 'boos' suggests Latin 'bos'—the ox. The presence of sheep ('baas') and of the ass, together with the sounds of alpha and omega (implied in the spectators' ahs and ohs) suggest the presence of Christ in the context. German *der Böse* is the devil. (Meaning proliferates. Perhaps we are also meant to find in 'boos' a reference to Martin Boos (1762-1825), a Bavarian Catholic priest who started a movement closely allied to Lutheran pietism. Repeated accusations in the consistorial courts compelled him to return to Bavaria, where his enemies followed him. He was a sort of defeated priest as Richard III was a defeated king.)

Many of the theatres, actors, and impressarios that figure in *FW* are discussed in Fitzpatrick's book, though there is, of course, no certainty that Joyce took his information from this source:

THEATRES

Smock Alley, started by John Ogilby: 60.32, 105.27, 396.09
Crow Street: 105.27
Richard Daly took over the Smock Alley Theatre in 1781: 219.08, 221.08, 375.21-3, 526.18-20
Tate Wilkinson, popular comedian and manager of Smock Alley: 90.11, 241.18

Henry Mossop and Stranger Barry were rival actors in the Crow Street and Smock Alley theatres: 134.11, 184.21, 569.30. The rivalry between the theatres was so keen as to be mutually injurious, and was fanned by their respective patrons. For instance, Lord Mornington (266.11), father of the Duke of Wellington, induced Kane O'Hara to write *Midas*, made up of Dublin jokes and by-sayings, in opposition to the Italian *burletta* at Smock Alley. O'Hara may appear at 580.32 and 610.03. *Midas* is named several times: 158.07, 481.33, 482.04.

The Adelphi Theatre later became the Queen's: 219.14.

ACTORS

The following are among those who appear in both Fitzpatrick and *FW*: Booth, 32.36, 257.19; Robert Corry, 140.02, 372.28; Foote, 376.23; Granby, 569.36; Tom King and Phelps, 67.24-6; Norris, 311.35, 534.15, 557.02; Quin, 305.20; Ryan, 77.14, 288.F6; Isaac Sparkes ('the greatest favourite that ever trod the Irish boards'), 376.23; Woodward, 34.15, 189.24, 280.04.

A play called *The Romp* is mentioned: 164.15, 407.07, 440.04, 562.13.

Finally, an incident mentioned on p. 249 of Fitzpatrick seems to be the source of 32.29: In 1747 a gentleman named Kelly was ejected from the green-room. He had, in a state of intoxication, climbed from the pit to the stage and insulted one of the ladies of the company. By this, the manager, Sheridan, incurred the odium of the 'young bloods' of the city, who, on the following Thursday, stormed the stage and green-rooms; the manager had to stay home. Kelly was sentenced to three months' imprisonment and a fine. The relevance of the incident to the whole *FW* myth is immediately obvious. Kelly is also named at 193.24, 299.27, 361.16, 407.16.

Fritz Senn

Every Klitty of a scolderymeid:
Sexual-Political Analogies

Hightime is ups be it down into outs according! When there shall be foods for vermin as full as feeds for the fett, eat on earth as there's hot in oven. When every Klitty of a scolderymeid shall hold every yardscullion's right to stimm her uprecht for whimsoever, whether on privates, whather in publics. And when all us romance catholeens shall have ones for all amanseprated. And the world is maidfree. (239.16-22)

These words form part of the resonant close to which the flower-girls have brought the address to Stainusless-Chuff-Shaun which they began on page 237. Their peroration continues the religious theme of the Annunciation, combined with longings for political rights and manifest demands for more scope in their sexual lives. They have their own annunciation to make.

Basically they are still reciting the Angelus-prayer and embroidering it with their own glosses. The prayer begins at 237.19: 'can ceive . . . from your holy post' and it continues until at least 239.25: 'he dwellst amongst us here's nobody knows save Mary.' The word 'knows' (again in 'mearing unknown', 239.30) is an apt one, retaining some of its biblical sense and referring us also to Mary's 'seeing I know not a man' (Luke 1:34). In the Old Testament 'to know' is often a more explicitly carnal verb. Knowledge is thought to be dangerous and corrupting in the legend of the fall of Adam and Eve no less than in *FW*. (The most conspicuous example in the latter is, of course, the initiation into the knowledge of geometry in II.2.) Correspondingly, sweet Stainusless is 'Pattern of our unschoold' (237.13), patron of the girls' innocence (Ger. *Unschuld*). This implies that to be schooled in knowledge amounts to losing one's innocence. Since the Floras attend 'St. Bride's Finishing Establishment' (220.03) they are, in fact, schooled. Their knowledge tends to be carnal and they betray their knowingness in multiple ways. The first sentence already shows the ambivalence of their complex feelings:

Hightime is ups be it down into outs according!

This may express their womanly submission in the words of the Virgin Mary to her Lord and Heavenly Husband: 'Be it done unto me according

27

to thy word' (Joyce's wording follows the text of the Angelus rather than either the Authorized or the Douai versions of Luke 1:38). Alternatively, it may mean that the girls devoutly assume the priest's role by echoing St Paul, himself a great believer in womanly submission: ' . . . now it is high time to awake out of sleep', words which follow his enumeration of some of the commandments and his upholding of love as the fulfilment of the law. Furthermore, 'it is high time' precedes St Paul's assurance that 'now is our salvation nearer than when we believed' (Rom. 13:9-11; cf. 'romance', 239.21). The girls have their own notion about this fulfilling love and they see the imminent salvation coloured by their own knowledge.

At the political level, 'it is high time' is a phrase we are used to hearing before the advocation of some reform. Reforms and political awakenings menace those who hold power. The sentence may be read as a defiant threat towards the adored idol himself: 'Thy time is up, thou art down and out', a theme which resounds throughout *FW*.

In a way, Chuff's time is indeed up. As an angel, 'coelicola' and 'deliverer of softmissives' (237.13), he is Gabriel, the bringer of the Lord's heavenly message. But significantly the girls, while emulating the Virgin, suppress the phrase 'to thy word' from their response. In its place they substitute their own words for the celestial (and male) commands. Shaun's habitual role is not Gabriel, however, but Michael, though even in this chief archangelic function he is hardly more successful in the present context. At the opening of the chapter's action Mick-Michael's 'soard fleshed light like likening' (222.22). Now he seems to have lost his sword, just as Gabriel's word has been taken from him. The girls, in hailing a ridiculous Caesar with the traditional formula ('we herehear, aboutobloss, O coelicola, thee salutamt', 237.12) profess themselves gladiators. As their name indicates, gladiators carry swords, which are not only weapons but also symbols of male power, both political and sexual.

If it is literally translated into German (the passage is rich in German words), 'Hightime' provides a further clue to what is really in the girls' minds: *Hochzeit* = wedding. Marriage seems to be the prime object. As a matter of fact, only a few lines earlier they rather equivocally repudiated the idea of marriage, using the same German word: 'No more hoaxites!' (239.12). *Hochzeit* recurs, associated with HCE, at 548.09: 'I was her hochsized, her cleavunto, her everest' (cf. Gen. 2:24). It also occupies Nuvoletta's optimistic mind in 'his glaubering hochskied' (157.11), though she is not overly fond of St Paul: 'she was overclused when Kneesknobs on his zwivvel was makeacting such a paulse of himshelp' (157.12).

28

For females whose temperature runs as high as is suggested in the course of the following sentence ('hot in oven') it may be better to marry than to burn, and for some of them, moreover, it may be high time to find a husband. But the girls hardly seem to be satisfied with a mere domestic ideal and they soon go one step further by agitating for no less than free love in all respects. The ups and downs and ins and outs are as erotic as they are political.

The desired future state is evoked in the second sentence:

> When there shall be foods for vermin as full as feeds for the fett, eat on earth as there's hot in oven.

This is not St Paul's idea of salvation nor is it quite the spirit of the Lord's Prayer, a faint echo of which may already have been detected in 'be it down'. The prayer is loudly if profanely uttered in 'eat on earth as there's hot in oven'. What the girls promise is a very earthy sort of paradise with an almost intra-uterine supply of food and warmth, and characterized by a cheap kind of socialism, offering votes for women and *panem et circenses*, food, fads,[1] and fêtes.

An echo of this wished-for elysium is introduced into the fable of the Ondt and the Gracehoper: '... an artsaccord ... A high old tide for the barheated publics and the whole day as gratiis! Fudder and lighting for ally looty ...' (415.17). Here, too, the social postulates comprise warmth and food supplied free, and they are expressed in a Germanicized vocabulary. The words 'high old tide' refer back to 'Hightime'. And the well-fed vermin seem to have proliferated to become the ubiquitous crawling insects of the fable.

In contrast to the fulfilment of infantile wishes and the attainment of general welfare and equal rights, 'foods for vermin' suggests a rotting corpse, while 'feed for the fett' reads like a Darwinian struggle for survival (Ger. *Fehde*—'feed'—means struggle). But it is those who are already fat who get more to eat and thus prove themselves the fittest. The German word *Fett* (grease, fat) together with 'full', brings us back to the Virgin Mary and the Angelus, for at 214.18 she is hailed by the washerwoman: 'Lord help you, Maria, full of grease, the load is with me!' We are aware that the load Mary bears in her womb will be eaten on earth in the Eucharist, while both the foetus and the bread are united in the common expression 'a bun in the oven' ('hot in oven').

The substitution of 'vermin' for 'women' reveals some basic uncertainty, vestiges perhaps of Pauline, puritanical notions of women as low and dirty. It also brings to mind 'Brandnew world. No stimulants and votes

---

[1] It is just possible to read Joyce's first version of this as 'fads for the fett' (Brit. Mus. Add. MS 47477, f. 36) on the microfilms.

for the bitches' in *A Portrait*.[2] Bitches and vermin are fertile. In *Stephen Hero* Stephen 'reviewed the plague of Catholicism. He seemed to see the vermin begotten in the catacombs in an age of sickness and cruelty . . . Like the plague of locusts . . .'[3]. He too is contemplating freedom and the forces that go to frustrate it:

> Exultation of the mind before joyful beauty, exultation of the body in free confederate labours, every natural impulse towards health and wisdom and happiness had been corroded by the pest of these vermin . . . He . . . would live his own life according to what he recognised as the voice of a new humanity, active, unafraid and unashamed.

While the gratifications the girls foresee are mainly oral, they are nonetheless sexual: 'oven' is slang for 'vagina' and 'uterus'; 'full as' may be turned into 'phallus'; 'foods' is phonetically very close to the Swiss-German vulgarism for 'cunt'[4], while 'vermin' sounds almost like the Swiss-German plural *Warmen*, commonly used for homosexuals.[5] Now, to supply vaginas to homosexuals, though it may be dear to some imaginations, provides no better solution for the world's sexual problems than the giving of food to the already fat does for its economic and political ones.

For the replacement of sex by food there is good psychoanalytical authority. In *The Interpretation of Dreams*,[6] Freud writes: 'Since "bed and board" (*mensa et thorus*) constitute marriage, in dreams the latter is often substituted for the former, and as far as practicable the sexual representation-complex is transposed to the eating-complex.'[7] On page 245, discussing sexual symbols, Freud provides a relevant gloss on 'vermin': 'Small animals and vermin are substitutes for little children, e.g. undesired sisters or brothers. To be infected with vermin is often the equivalent for pregnancy.' A curious ring is thus given to the miraculous pregnancy

---

[2] *A Portrait*, 'Definitive Text', New York 1964, 195.09.

[3] *Stephen Hero*, New York 1955, 194.04.

[4] The same word seems to contribute to the meaning of 'a footsey kungoloo' (131.35), 'Foots!' (501.07), 'Bennydick hotfoots onimpudent stayers!' (469.23), and 'For my own coant! She has studied! Piscisvendolor! You're grace! Futs dronk of Wouldndom!' (408.35).

[5] Joyce makes undisguised use of the word in 'fram choicest of wiles with warmen and sogns' (596.07): If war-men are women, there is a suspicion of homosexuality ('wiles' could be Oscar Wilde). The inversion of 'phallus' into 'full as' might also suggest sexual inversion.

[6] Sigmund Freud, *The Interpretation of Dreams*, trans. A. A. Brill. Modern Library, New York 1950, p. 243.

[7] The echo 'eatupus complex' (128.36) in an already undoubtedly Freudian allusion would seem a neat confirmation that Joyce did in fact make use of Brill's translation.

of the Virgin, just as the exuberant and life-affirming joy of the Annunciation is perhaps grimly set off against Swift's contemptuous reference to 'the most pernicious race of little odious vermin'.[8]

To cast doubt on the purity of the Virgin's motives there is no need for the girls to look further than the pages of the Bible: 'hot in oven' recalls 'They are all adulterers, as an oven heated by the baker . . . They are all hot as an oven . . . ' (Hosea 7:4, 7). The Hebrew prophet Hosea, who reviled the sins of Israel, had some personal experience of marriage: he married 'a wife of whoredoms' and 'an adulteress' (Hosea 1:2, 3:1). Hosea means 'a saviour', as the Douai Bible explains, and the saviour is one of Shaun's favourite roles. In the Douai Bible as in the French the prophet's name is given as Osee; the girls' words are not only Hosea's, they are also *osées*.

Joyce often associated food and eating with Switzerland, as I tried to show in 'Some Zurich Allusions in *FW*'.[9] This link may also justify the many Swiss references in our passage. In the third sentence the women again strike a Swiss-German note in their demands for equal rights:

> When every Klitty of a scolderymeid shall hold every yardscullion's right to stimm her uprecht for whimsoever, whether on privates, whather in publics.

Up to the present, the Swiss women are almost the only ones who have asked in vain for the right to vote—*Stimmrecht*, as it is called in Switzerland (literally, the right to raise one's voice). They may—and do—of course raise their voices, as do the girls in the present context. The usual argument deployed against the women by their menfolk is that they, being dependent and politically immature ('but yours in ammatures', 239.11), would in any case rely on their husbands' or relatives' judgement, or vote according to whim or wheather for whimsoever. And so the sentence may be read as a counterpoint of the women's clamours and the men's ironic comments on the possibility of their voting. One of the most common assertions is, of course, that women should stick to home and kitchen.

In *FW* the kitchen is Kate's domain. It is she who usually occupies the stage after the men have fought their battles. Here Klitty or Cathleen wants to fight her own battles—with the men, or against them. Not every Klitty is as lucky as Kitty of Coleraine, the dairymaid in the ballad, who won kisses when she broke her pitcher. Kate is an old maid, cold and frigid, and given to scolding. A 'scold', the *S.O.E.D.* informs us, can be 'a person (esp. a woman) of ribald speech'. Ribald the speech

---

[8] Last sentence of Chapter VI of 'A Voyage to Brobdingnag'.

[9] *The Analyst*, XIX, December 1960.

certainly is, and it needs little ingenuity to discover that Klitty's desire to take part in masculine affairs is a barely disguised yearning for sexual favours and for the general licence which is more commonly allowed to men. The uprightness ('her uprecht') is clearly more phallic than moral (though Ruprecht is also the name of a Bavarian saint) and most of the words used have blatantly sexual overtones. Long ago Freud established a connexion between the kitchen and sexuality in dreams: 'But the groups of ideas appertaining to plant-life, or to the kitchen, are just as often chosen to conceal sexual images ... The ugliest as well as the most intimate details of sexual life may be thought or dreamed of in apparently innocent allusions to culinary operations, and the symptoms of hysteria will become absolutely unintelligible if we forget that sexual symbolism may conceal itself behind the most commonplace and inconspicuous matters as its safest hiding-place.'[10] Freud then goes on to quote, and analyse, a dream which might well have furnished Joyce with some words (my italics) for his incredibly complex involutions. The dream is called 'the flower-dream' of a female patient:

> Preliminary dream: She goes to the two *maids* in the *kitchen* and *scolds* them for taking so long to prepare 'a little bite of *food*.' She also sees a very large number of heavy *kitchen* utensils in the *kitchen*, heaped into piles and turned *upside down* in order to drain. Later addition: The two *maids* go down to fetch *water*, and have, as it were, to climb into a river which reaches up to the house or into the court*yard*.[11]

In the subsequent 'main dream' cherry-blossoms, camellias, and bunches of hair are explained sexually and may be compared to 'Cattie Hayre and tip Carminia to tap La Chérie' (239.24). A big branch that the dreamer is 'carrying ... in her *hand*' is likened, in Freud's footnote, to the lily-*stem* that the angel bears at the Annunciation. Freud's pointing out that he will 'print in *Roman* type everything which is to be sexually interpreted' may or may not add a nice touch to why the girls call themselves, in the next sentence, 'romance catholeens'.[12]

It is not easy to specify what exactly the girls seem to have in mind. A host of interpretations suggest themselves, all indelicate.[13] Perhaps we

[10] Freud, *The Interpretation of Dreams*, p. 235.

[11] Freud, ibid., p. 236.

[12] Freud, ibid., pp. 236-7.

[13] After publication of my notes on Klitty in the *Newslitter* a suggestion by J. D. Stowell (*AWN* 4:1, *AWN* 5:4) that 'stimm' = Ger. *stemmen* = 'fuck' aroused a certain amount of controversy, extending particularly into private correspondence. I am not myself aware of any such meaning in the German verb. But even without it the obscenity of the sentence is dominant enough, and I was surprised to have pointed out to me the sexual, genital or urinatory meanings of certain words which I had taken for granted: apart from clitoris they are: yard, cul, cullion, stem(s), upright, whim, the privates, wet, whet, water.

are being told of an old maid's right to stimulate herself, or of her right to use every scullion's or rascal's hand for the same or a similar purpose. Even a layman may feel justified in bringing what knowledge he has of penis-envy and similar findings of the psychoanalytical school to bear on the passage. The suggestion of 'clitoris' in 'Klitty' is the basis of some analogizing: women are striving after political activity, a prerogative of men: the clitoris is a female counterpart of the male member (cf. 585.26: 'Withdraw your member! Closure. This chamber stands abjourned.'). If we keep for the moment to etymology and turn up the derivation of clitoris we find that it comes from a Greek verb meaning—in ironic contrast to the girls' vociferations—to shut up (cf. 'Closure', *above*).

Scatology is involved, along with sexuality and politics (often held to be dirty, anyway). The girls ask for the same public facilities for making water as are available to men. Mrs Ruth von Phul has kindly drawn my attention to a further analogy:

> In the unabridged edition of Havelock Ellis's *Studies in the Psychology of Sex* you will find his indignant comments on the lack of public conveniences for women at the turn of the century in England. The result, says Ellis, was that many gentlewomen were forced to learn to relieve themselves upright, in public, shielded only by the long full skirts of the period. Ellis seems to have been equally fascinated by female micturition as Joyce was. Ellis's informants—or some of them—found it titillating, even exciting, to urinate thus publicly. By the time Joyce wrote the *Wake*, both the campaign to install public WC's for women of the British Isles and the suffrage movement had succeeded, but to the Dublin girls of 1900-04 both the vote and the toilets were Utopian dreams. But even at the time the conventions bound only those who had pretensions to gentility; scullery maids or peasants could make water in public, if the whim struck them, standing like boys. And the poor prostitute who could not take her client to a private room, or even a bed, had to entertain him and receive the "yardscullion" standing, outdoors, in public, against a wall or in a corner.[14]

The presence of the micturating girls and (reading the word 'privates' in another sense) the three soldiers of the Phoenix Park, may remind us of the ever-present troubles of HCE (*hold every yardscullion's*). The Swiss-German reading of 'foods for vermin' reinforces the idea that the soldiers are homosexual (or vices reversed), which adds still further to HCE's bother.

All this may, of course, be interpreted in a more decorous sense. We may choose to find here, simply, an old maid's (or young girl's) hope of

---

[14] Mrs von Phul in a private letter to me.

holding a husband's right hand,[15] either at the wedding ceremony, as a claim to social status, or in order to share in some of his activities. In Switzerland there are still cantons where voting is carried out in public by holding up one's right hand ('talking of plebiscites by a show of hands', 523.05). Joyce's spelling of -meid contains German *Eid*, oath. This may be the oath of marriage, and it is also a hint that the Swiss confederation (*Eid*genossenschaft) is based on an oath. The verb *meiden* means to avoid; one does become an old maid by avoiding certain perils, or attractions, of life. 'Klitty' is close to Dutch *klit* and German *Klette*, both meaning 'burr' and suggesting the tenacity of women. As it happens, *clit* is also an Irish word meaning—'the desire for copulation in swine'.

In a mood of frustration and jealousy Stephen Dedalus in the *Portrait* thinks of the 'church which was the scullerymaid of christendom'.[16] Klitty, the scolderymeid, who soon becomes 'catholeens', is also the Catholic Church in Ireland—a church well known for its scolding interference and for its insistence on having a say in politics, in which it has been markedly successful.

Another parallel between the church and the kitchen occurs in 'Grace': Mrs Kernan's 'faith was bounded by her kitchen but, if she was put to it, she could believe also in the banshee and in the Holy Ghost'.[17]

All the foregoing themes are further developed in the next sentence:

And when all us romance catholeens shall have ones for all amanseprated.

'And when all us . . . ' sounds like a defiant rhetorical phrase in German: '*Und wenn alles . . .* ' (and if everything . . .). The emancipation of women is given an Irish twist and combined with the emancipation of the Roman Catholics. Catholic emancipation is the achievement of Daniel O'Connell, the Liberator. Chuff, as a 'deliverer' (237.13), is a liberator too. O'Connell is known also for the many bastards he left behind him. His wife's Christian name was Mary. Romantic notions about ancient Ireland are set off against the shock experienced by pious patriots when faced with Yeats' representation of the Countess Cathleen. There may well be an intimation, too, of Parnell's fight for Home Rule (which is always to be taken as a dispute about who is to rule in the home as well): Klitty-Cathleen is Kitty O'Shea, who exercised a decided influence on Irish politics and was the cause of the Irish Catholics' separating themselves from Parnell. Quite a bit of Ireland's struggle to gain her freedom is thus squeezed into a short sentence, but the context suggests that 'ones for all'

[15] 'The left may signify homosexuality, incest and perversion, while the right signifies marriage, relations with a prostitute etc.' Freud, *The Interpretation of Dreams*, p. 245.

[16] *A Portrait*, 220.17.

[17] *Dubliners*, ed. R. Scholes. London 1967, p. 178; New York 1968, p. 158.

may refer to the historical-political motto of Switzerland: *Einer für alle, alle für einen*. The motto reminds us of Switzerland's own fight for independence, which succeeded long before the Irish one (with the exception, of course, of the women's franchise).

Pure Irish girls (Catherine from Gr. *katharos*, pure) will have the hero-lovers they read about in romances or novels. But Izzy, in the following chapter (II.2), sees romance in a different light; her first footnote begins: 'Rawmeash, quoshe with her girlic teangue' (260.F1). 'Rawmaush' or 'rawmaish' is an Anglo-Irish word meaning the same, roughly, as German *Quatsch* ('quoshe'): 'romance or fiction, commonly applied to foolish senseless brainless talk (Ir. *ramas* from romance)'.[18] Rawmeash may suggest Romeo, but it is nearer to raw meat than to airily romantic conceptions. Romantic or not, the girls dream about the separate man they will each of them have, with a manse to prate in. They may wish to separate a man from another woman, but in any case they will all want some kind of *amans* (Lat. = lover). The clause ' . . . will have a man separated' is an answer to the motto of the Most Illustrious Order of St Patrick: *Quis separabit*—Who shall separate us? (255.35, 625.07; *see also* 585.24). The girls from St Bride's school, wishing to break up the political and social order made by man, are boosting the female patron saint of Ireland at the expense of St Patrick. *Femina separabit*. The Celtic goddess Brigit ('bright elects', 239.28) was less holy than the Christian saint she later became: she was a goddess of fire and the hearth ('earth', 239.17, read 'hearth' in the first draft). St Bridget was known as 'Mary of the Gael'. Similarly, the Virgin Mary, the heavenly bride, could be said to be breaking into the all-too-male and all-too-holy Trinity.

There is, too, a St Bridget of Sweden who founded the order of the Brigittines. Her daughter was also canonized: St Catherine of Sweden. Yet another St Catherine, of Siena, a pure maiden, is said to be noted for her immense love for Jesus. She was instrumental in bringing back the popes from Avignon to Rome and was thus a politically active woman.

In a less saintly spirit we could again read 'When all we girls will have a man, Sepp, rated'. Sepp is the common Swiss short form of Joseph. The scolding maids would naturally have little sympathy with the notoriously chaste Joseph,[19] and men of his stamp will have to be avoided.

---

[18] The information is to be found in P. W. Joyce, *English As We Speak It in Ireland*. London and Dublin, 1910.

[19] Joseph and Mary, together with an echo of 'votes for women', turn up a few pages later: 'Luiz-Marios Josephs . . . to be offered up missas for vowts for widders' (243.35). It is not easy to disentangle the two sexes, Napoleon's wives have become males, and so has Maria. Giuseppe Mario was a tenor whose voice made him famous. The widows in 'vowts for widders' seem to be endowed with strong male aggressive impulses: a *Widder*, in German, is a ram.

The other Joseph of biblical fame, the provider of food for the Egyptians, was coveted by at least one female.

In *Ulysses* Bloom and Molly are Joseph and Mary, and these parallels help to give more depth to the passage. Molly has managed to take lovers. In Bloom's mind the chance phrase 'For him!', drawn from an erotic novel, becomes associated with her recent lover Hugh Boylan, whom Molly got to know because of the qualities of her voice ('stimm ... for whimsoever'). Bloom, like a scullion, begins and ends his day pottering in the kitchen; he is accused of an impropriety with a scullery-maid named Mary; he is concerned about public facilities for women.

Such is the overdetermination of Joyce's words that we may be tempted to break up 'catholeens' into 'cat', 'hole', and 'ens': woman as a catlike entity ('cat' may mean 'harlot' or even 'vagina'—'Cattie Hayre', 239.24), with a hole (which also doubles with 'whole', totality), who is saddled, moreover, with the obsolete burden of suffering (to thole). We may also see in 'romance catholeens' a summation of practically all the girls' desires in the person of Catherine II, Empress of Russia. She was one of the Romanoffs, had a weak husband, and herself took over the responsibility and honour of ruling firmly and successfully. She earned for herself the title of greatness—but she is equally renowned and perhaps envied for her many sexual exploits.

This digression into Russian history may have been prepared for us by the closing words of the preceding paragraph: 'Vania, Vania Vaniorum, Domne Vanias!' (239.14). Vania is a short form of the Russian name Ivan (= Shaun). This constitutes, perhaps, a secondary reference to Ivan VI who should have become Tsar but was imprisoned and murdered in the second year of Catherine's reign. Fittingly, for a chapter which deals, at the surface-level, with children at play, both Ivan and Catherine appear in diminutive forms: Vania, Catholeen.

Catherine II was emancipated in other respects too: she wrote a play about the legendary Russian hero Oleg, one of the early rulers. Oleg is mentioned along with his predecessor, Askold (310.16).[20] It is just possible that Askold appears disguised in '*a scold*erymeid', with yet another change of sex. Catherine was of German origin, which may form a further justification for the use of so many (Swiss) German expressions (cf. also Fr. *allemand* in 'all amans-').

It is now possible to see another reference to a politically prominent woman in an earlier allusion: 'eat on' might take in Margaret O'Neill Eaton (or Peggy O'Neill) the daughter of a Washington pub-keeper, noted for her beauty, wit and vivacity. In her second marriage she became

[20] *See Second Census* and *JJR*, vol. 2, nos 1-2, Spring-Summer 1958, p. 63.

the wife of a politician who was appointed Secretary of War under President Jackson. This did not suit the spouses of some high officials who charged Mrs Eaton with improper conduct before her marriage. Partly for this reason the cabinet was reorganized (one of President Jackson's cabinets at the time being nicknamed the 'kitchen cabinet'). All in all, Mrs Eaton caused quite a stir in politics and does not seem to have done too badly in matrimony, for she married a third time and was able to catch a young Italian dancing master when she was herself by no means youthful.

Not all the women brought together here in a few lines were equally successful. To return to Ireland, the legendary Kathleen who pursued St Kevin was rejected. Shaun often plays the part of St Kevin, especially in Book IV. There 'Kathlins is kitchin' (601.32). At Glendalough St Kevin's church is called St Kevin's Kitchen. In the words of Thomas Moore:

> ... the good Saint little knew
> What that wily sex can do ...
> But nor earth nor heaven is free
> From her power, if fond she be.[21]

The heroine of one of the Ossianic poems, Cathlin of Clutha, disguises herself as a warrior and takes part in the fighting. She appears at 329.15. Further warriors in *Ossian*, real males, have names like Cathol and Cathul. Joyce may not be referring to either of these characters,[22] but there were enough sources available to make him aware that in Irish names and words the syllable 'Cath-' often means battle (*cat* in modern Irish). The militant nature of the girls is thus stressed.

By these various and ambiguous emancipations 'the world is maid-free'. Not only has the political liberation taken a definitely sexual turn,

---

[21] Thomas Moore. 'By that lake, whose gloomy shore ...'

[22] There are frequent quotations from *Ossian* in II.1, but most of them were added at a later stage on the galleys. One of Macpherson's original footnotes, to be found in vol. II, p. 204 of *Ossian*, 1762, but left out of many subsequent editions, might be of some relevance. Even if it were purely coincidental, the allusion is too delightful to be missed:

> Religious, however, as this poet was, he was not altogether decent, in the scenes he introduces between Swaran and the wife of Congcullion, both of whom he represents as giants. It happening unfortunately, that Congcullion was only of a moderate stature, his wife, without hesitation, preferred Swaran, as a more adequate match for her own gigantic size. From this fatal preference proceeded so much mischief, that the good poet altogether lost sight of his principal action, and he ends the piece, with an advice to men, in the choice of wives, which, however good it may be, I shall leave concealed in the obscurity of the original.

—Congcullion might have become 'yardscullion's', in keeping with the general tenor of the passage; the quasi-vaginal 'con-g' would have been replaced by phallic 'yard' (also indicative of remarkable size). The note refers to the poem '*Cath*-Loda'.

but the girls also make free with the idea of the Word being made Flesh —though their conception of how this is to come to pass is not an immaculate one. But, theologically, it is Christ, the Word Incarnate, who will free the world, and as he is said to be the heavenly bridegroom of maiden nuns, he makes the world maid-free in a more respectable sense. Our girls are brides too, 'these bright elects' (239.28)—the right to vote entails the right to be elected. When Jaun delivers his sermon to the girls of St Bride's he poses as a heavenly bridegroom and a desirable Don Juan. He then takes the opportunity to pay them back in kind by twisting their own words into an unctuous exhortation, the undertones of which are no less lascivious: 'Never let the promising hand usemake free of your oncemaid sacral.' (433.27.)

But Joyce himself appears to be paying back an opponent in his own words. In *Time and Western Man* Wyndham Lewis attacked Joyce and others for upholding time: 'Hightime is ups.' Lewis calls his first chapter 'Some of the Meanings of Romance', and one of its earliest sentences reads: 'Christianity has been, for the European, strictly speaking, a *romance*.'[23] Joyce, too, gives us some of the meanings of romance. We may also hear an echo of Lewis' 'the wholesale changeover of what was "public" into what . . . was private.'[24] On page 15 Lewis writes: 'Where Romance enters the sphere of morals it is at the gate of sex . . . It is even extremely easy in the modern West to *sexify* everything . . .'. Joyce was not slow to take up the hint—applying it not only to this passage but also to the very title of Lewis' book (292.06). The following extract from *Time and Western Man* must have been considered by Joyce as yet another quarry where he could find, or re-find, most of his raw material:

> . . . advancing any kitchen-maid's sickly gushed-out romance, provided she only calls her baby-boy her 'bastard', and can be patronized (by himself and the reading-crowd he addresses) because he has never learnt how to spell, and so can be discovered, as you discover things in disused lofts or in gutters, or in that case a scullery . . . [25]

Fritz Senn

[23] P. Wyndham Lewis, *Time and Western Man*. Boston 1957, p. 3.
[24] Ibid., p. 14.
[25] 'The Revolutionary Simpleton', *Time and Western Man*, p. 29.

II   Linguistic Studies

French Argot in *Finnegans Wake*

~~~~~~

Joyce had a copy of Olivier Leroy's *Dictionary of French Slang*, London 1935. This book is now in the Lockwood Memorial Library at Buffalo, and is catalogued as No. 179 in Professor Thomas E. Connolly's *Descriptive Bibliography of the Personal Library of James Joyce*, University of Buffalo, 1955.

This provides a convenient source-book for Joyce's use of some French slang, even if it was not always Joyce's actual source. I have made the following list as short as possible, excluding doubtful words. The word given first, in italics, is from Leroy, as is the explanation (sometimes abbreviated) that follows. Its occurrence in *FW* is given after the full stop.

appels, faire des appels, to make amorous overtures. appelled, 606.32

arranger, to spoil, demolish, wound. arronged orranged, 203.27

baba, babafier, astounded, to astound. Baba-..., 3.15; Bababadkessy, 471.02; babad, 534.10; babazounded, 552.28

bamban, nickname for a lame person. Bambam's bonniest, 389.12 (with Banba, Ireland)

bath, good, tip-top. Beauty's bath, 355.13 (with 'Beauty of Bath', an apple)

betterave, nose, esp. big and red like a beetroot. betteraved, 164.28

biffe, trade of a rag picker. biff, 23.34

Boum, voilà!, said by a waiter to mean that he has heard the customer's call. Boumce, 370.30. (Here the bar window drops before the waiter can say '*voilà*'—it is closing time, or 'Es ist Polizeistunde': 370.30.)

chouchou, darling, favourite; *chouchouter*, to fondle. choochoo, 538.19

foin, tobacco. Foinn, 343.25

frick, money, expense. Frick's Flame, 537.30

gau, crab louse. Gau, 233.27

ginginer, to ogle; *ginginer les hanches*, to walk swaying the hips. gingin, 116.19

mou, human flesh, body. mou, 267.22, 562.26

orange, avoir des oranges à l'étalage, sur son étagère, (of a woman) to have a full breast. orangeray, 246.26

Paname, Paris. Paname-, 228.22

pante, name given by swindlers to their prospective victims. *pante blanche*, 370.06

perroquet, *étrangler un perroquet*, (lit. to strangle a parrot) to drink an absinthe (from its green colour). Strangler of soffiacated green parrots, 534.27

piger, to understand, to get nabbed. *Pige pas*, 272.L1

Pitou, French soldier (esp. green from the country). pitounette, 143.32

platine, *avoir une platine*, to have the gift of the gab. platinism, 164.11

poisse, 1. bad luck; 2. ponce; *poisser*, 1. to steal; 2. to be caught, get nabbed; 3. to be boring (*tu nous poisses*, you're getting on our nerves). Poisse!, 177.12 (all the given meanings seem to be implied)

pomper, to drink, to booze. Pompery, 64.15

rondin, woman's breast. rondinelles, 359.29

rosse, rotter. Rosse, 391.30

Saint-Lago (=*Saint-Lazare*), prison where prostitutes were kept. lagos, 203.08

tam-tam, *faire du tam-tam*, to kick up a row. tamtammers, 27.20

tapette, *avoir une fière tapette*, to be a chatterbox. tapette, 79.23

trou, a hole of a place; *boire comme un trou*, to drink like a fish. trou Normend fashion, 510.20

truquer, to fake. *Truckeys' cant*, 282.L2.

James S. Atherton

Kiswahili Words in *Finnegans Wake*

"That was kissuahealing with bantur for balm!" (204.3-4)

198.11 nyumba noo, chamba choo. Nyumba = house; noo = a large whetstone; chamba = a hiding place, also, to wash one's private parts (said of a woman); choo = privy: Joyce found "choo" particularly appropriate for what it names, since it contains the German symbol "oo." (Because of the alliteration and parallel construction, and the nonsense nature of the sequence, I think it is reasonable (among reasonable men) to say that in this case Joyce used the words with little or no consideration for their sense, though the meanings are significant, if not particularly so in the case of "nyumba." *The words "noo" and "chamba" are the only ones which do not appear at all in his notes* (Buffalo MS VI.B.46, "Kissahueli"). (Cf. the sequence at -.5, based on rivers.)

198.16 sina feza = I have no money

198.16 The words "me" and "him," substituting the objective case for the subjective, are familiar native-sounding talk. I think, however, that Joyce consciously based them on K. pronouns, which combine the cases into one form. "Mimi" (or, as frequently abbreviated, "mi") = I, me; "yeye" = he, him/she, her.

198.16 absantee. This appears in the notes as "absanthe (thanks)," and it is a mistake: the "b" should be an "h." The error in reverse was made in another entry but caught: in setting down the words for silver and gold he wrote "zalahu," then followed it with the correct "zahabu" (gold).

199.12 Wendawanda, a fingerthick. Wanda = a finger's breadth or thickness. It is the Swahili inch. In his notes Joyce wrote "1 fingerthick." He was working from a German source (*see below*), and it must have said "fingerdick," as in Velten's definition: "Breite oder Dicke eines Fingers, fingerdick."

199.16 yayis. Yayi = egg

199.20 hamjambo, bana? A K. greeting, "Hujambo, bana?", roughly analogous to Eng. "How are you, sir?" "Hamjambo" means

43

"are you (pl.), etc.," which does not agree with the singular "bana." I cannot say whether Joyce knew this; there is of course a pun with Eng. "ham," but the "m" appears in the notes as well.

Though this fits the pattern in no particular, there is a reference to the running "How are you today, my dark sir?"'s which appear in so many languages. K. itself supplies the "dark," being a Negersprache.

201.23 homa = fever

201.24 mahun of the horse. The phrase "man of the horse" occurs in the notes, but I am unable to state its relationship to K.—if it has one. It is not a literal translation of K. "horseman," for example. Earlier in the notes there is a brief exercise in genitives ("days of the work, the werks day"—"werks" being German), and presumably the same thing is being got at in both.

201.25 bundukiboi meet askarigal. Bunduki = gun; boi = houseboy, servant (derived from Eng. "boy"); askari = soldier

201.30 meanacuminamoyas. mia na kumi na moja = correct K. for the number 111 (lit., (one)hundred and ten and one, or, more correctly, (one)hundred and eleven, since "kumi na moja" = eleven)

203.31 But the majik wavus has elfun anon meshes. Maji = water; wavu = net, as a fishnet ("meshes"); elfu = 1000. Note the pattern: one letter is added to the end of each K. word.

203.32 Simba ... Oga. Simba = lion; "Oga" is a problem. In his notes Joyce wrote "ogakoga (bath)." "Oga" is the short form of "koga," "to bathe," and, as "oga," is indistinguishable except in context from "oga" meaning "fear, cowardice." "Oga" does not mean "bath," but Joyce thought it did, and we therefore read it "bath," a waterword in a waterchapter.

204.21 Mtu or Mti. Mtu = man; mti = tree. K. for "river" is "mto," which does not appear in the notes. "Tum" and "Tim" skirt "Tom," making 2 + 1 'witnesses.'

206.28 pooleypooley. Polipoli = slowly

209.11 tembo = palmwine (v. 428.1); tumbo = belly (Ger. "bauch" in the notes, followed by "utumbo (bowels)" and preceded by a word for "lung"); pilipili = pepper; saa = watch, clock, hour (Ger. "uhr" in the notes); taa = lamp; bizaa = merchandise (v. 210.2), but in his notes Joyce wrote "bizari," "spice" (pilipili and bizari are two of the three chief parts of their curry powder), and this word and meaning is preserved by the preceding "specis"

—under a vowel exchange, "spices." Considering the language involved, I believe the case of "bizaas" is the most staggering I have ever come upon.

My K. list originally appeared in *WN* 12, p. 8. After reading Joyce's notes I was able to drop seven second and third definitions as superfluous ("nyumba = house, hut" now appears "nyumba = house," and so on), spell "polipoli" for "polepole" (the "pooleypooley" of the text could indicate either), discover the appropriateness of "choo" (at the time I wrote I did not know the German "oo" anyway), add the incorrect "absantee," redefine "oga" incorrectly to be correct, and crack "specis bizaas."

It was a list by Herr Philipp Wolff of Basel (*WN* 8) which occasioned my paper. Outside *ALP* Herr Wolff was reduced to dragging in such incredible rubbish that I assumed there was no further K. It was a gamble I lost. There are six words on p. 237, in a chapter which I will not research for a time yet. In any case, three of the words appear incorrectly—two of the errors a typist's fault, one Joyce's—and this makes it rough hunting for anyone. As almost always, Joyce's mistake is written into the text and cannot be touched, but this is happily not the case with typists' errors. Here are the words:

237.15 our barnaboy, our chapachap. Barua = letter; chapa = stamp

In his notes Joyce wrote "barua (letter)," but the "u" was so totally ambiguous that he later read "barna." I believe Joyce's "u" and "n" are the most difficult letters to resolve if they come into question. They continually fooled his typists, even in the simplest words, but he usually caught the errors. In this instance he has written his own error into the text, and "barnaboy" it must be. (For considerably more discussion of this problem see footnote 3 and the paragraph to which it refers in my "Hardest Crux," *JJQ*, 1:3, Spring 1964.)

Emendation of "chepachap": In his notes Joyce wrote "chapa." He added ", our barnaboy, our chapachap," to galley (B.M. Add. MS 47477.283) and the typist copied "our barneboy, our chepachap," on -.282b (the back of the preceding galley sheet). "barneboy" was corrected but "chepachap" missed. The typist's error was the same in both cases, the misreading of "a" as "e."

237.30 The rains of Demani are masikal as of yere. Demani = springtime in East Africa, August to November (Joyce wrote "Sept Oct"); masika = fall in East Africa, March to May, the time of the great rains ("grosse Regenzeit"—Velten) (Joyce wrote "rains")

237.31 Baraza. Baraza = veranda

237.31 Siku of calmy days. Siku = day

   Emendation of "Siker": In his notes Joyce wrote "siku." He added "Siku" to galley (B.M. Add. MS 47477.283) and the typist copied "Siker" on -.282b (the back of the preceding galley sheet). The first stroke of the "u" was read as "e," the second as "r."

These words were added to the same galley at the same time. Much more remarkable is the fact that all of the *ALP* K. was added to one set of *FW* galleys, B.M. Add. MS 47476A.261-275. The addition of K. words, or phrases and sentences constructed around K. words, was to be Joyce's farewell to *ALP*. K. now stands (I think I am correct in this) as the third most important language in the most popular chapter of the book.

The source: "Words (apparently always of Arabic origin) which in English dictionaries and grammars of K. end in '-dha(a)' or '-tha(a)' are, in many German and French works, spelled '-za(a).' Thus Joyce's 'feza' and 'bizaa.' However, the variant 'bana' is common in German works and not in French. We therefore deduce a German source. . . ." This is what I wrote, and I was correct. The word "fingerthick" was another indication. The notes confirm my hypothesis, most obviously by the definition of "saa" as "uhr" and "tumbo" as "bauch." In these cases Joyce retained the German because it held in one word the several English definitions possible. Mainly because of the order of the notes, I am convinced that a grammar was the source except for "noo" and "chamba," and probably "bizaa," but I know of none which can be, or need be, proven the one. The "u" of "kissuahealing" is accounted for by the common German spelling "Kisuahili" or "Kisuaheli."

To read the epigraph it is necessary to know that K. is a member of the Bantu family of languages.

It is also a famous lingua franca. In *ALP* there is "franca langua" (198.18-19), Chinook (212.33), and Hindustani (198.18—"Honddu jarkon" = Hindu jargon, one of the common meanings of "jargon" being a lingua franca). To my former notes on this subject I can now add the fact that earlier in the same book Joyce took notes on "Beche La Mar" (*sic*—cf. Spielberg), another lingua franca. (Interestingly, with the aid of this list we discover that a lot of pidgin we would casually assume Chinese is in fact Pacific Islands, and it pops up all over the place. "You, you make what name?" (293.1-2), for example.)

Several of the languages mentioned in *ALP* have names with watery derivations. The root "Swahili" means "of the coasts" (Swahili folk live along the east coasts of Africa), the root "Hindu" is ultimately derived from Sanskrit "sindhu," meaning "river," esp. the Indus, and Hebrew

(198.19) means "one who is from across (the river)." (Appropriately, the latter appear with rivers, the Honddu and the Ebro.)

I would not want to indulge in special pleading for rather remote effects, but I do think it not accidental that K. is a lingua franca whose name has a watery derivation. To restate the above in concise form: The first K. words, seven of them, are found at 198.11 and 198.16: "Honddu jarkon" is at 198.18, "franca langua" at 198.18-19, Hebrew at 198.19. Only Chinook is missing, coming a little further from the end than these from the beginning.

N.B.: Material from the notes given with the permission of the Lockwood Memorial Library, State University of New York at Buffalo, and the Estate. Material from the British Museum MSS given with the permission of the Estate.

Jack P. Dalton

POSTSCRIPT

There is another K. word in *FW*, "radi" (23.7). It means "thunder." See Buffalo MS VI. B. 15.169.

In the previous version of this essay I wrote: "['Kisuahili'] was the preferred spelling in the early days of K. lexicography (v. Krapf (1882), for example . . .). The Germans have used 'Kisuaheli' and, less often, 'Kisuahili.' The important point is that Joyce clearly uses the older spelling, which by the late 30's was an archaic variant." This was poohpoohed. One gentleman stated that *he* had gone to school [in America] in the 1910's and had been taught "Swahili," not "Suahili." He also pointed out that the *OED* didn't record these variant spellings. He made a rude play on the name "Krapf." With such cogent arguments did he set at naught the clear evidence of *FW*'s "kissuahealing" (see the epigraph). Here is the last laugh: I have discovered two places where Joyce wrote down the name of this language. In each he wrote "Kisuaheli." See Buffalo MS VI. B. 15.169 and B.M. Add. MS 47488.180.

Finnegans Wake and
the Secret Languages of Ireland

~~~~~~

I am grateful to Mr John Kelleher for telling me to read *The Secret Languages of Ireland* by R. A. Macalister, Cambridge 1937. The book is great fun, and Joyce used it. The following words in Shelta, Ogham, Bog Latin, Bearlagair Na Saer, and Irish which occur in *FW* are just what I happened to notice. The Irish words are all explained by Macalister's book (and are included for that reason), but of course in this instance Joyce need not have used Macalister as a source. All the other words listed were, however, added to the text of *FW* soon after the date of publication of *The Secret Languages of Ireland*.

> Talking in riddles has been at all times a favourite amusement among the Celtic peoples.—*The Secret Languages of Ireland*, p. 73.

53.01	fin (and elsewhere) *fin* (Shelta) = man
59.24	Aratar *aratar* (Ir.) = plough
83.23	gamy *gami* (Shelta) = bad; (also *gammy* = common cant word for 'bad')
89.30, 32; 90.01-2; 223.04; 602.12 (?)	Ogma Sun-face (89-90 lists names of various Ogham-ciphers, taken from *The Secret Languages of Ireland*, pp. 47-8:)
89.30	Shirt-of-two-strokes Ogham
.30	Mac (or Son) Ogham—*see* Pig (Muc) Ogham, *below*
.30-31	Finn's-ladder Ogham (this had three forms)
.30-31	Finn's-three-shanked Ogham
.31	Head-in-a-bush Ogham
.31	Head-under-a-bush Ogham
.32	Serpent-through-the-heather Ogham
.32	Millrace Ogham
.33	Arm, Bird, Colour Oghams

48

.33   Defdum. Ogham is a language of signs and gestures, hence like the language of the deaf and dumb

.33   glomsk *glonsk* (Shelta) = man

.34   handy. Ogham is spoken with the hands

.34   Pig (Muc) Ogham (*see* Mac Ogham, *above*)

.34   jotalpheson ... jasons. Macalister explains (pp. 90-1) that in Bog Latin certain letters in Irish words are replaced by the name of the letter-of-the-alphabet in Irish. He says it is 'as if a Greek meaning Jason called him "Jotalphason".'

.35   ture as there's an ital on atac. True as there's a tail on a cat (Joyce is making up his own little word puzzles)

.36   hankowchaff. Ogham is a method of 'hand chaff'. By the association of Ogma Sun-face and Sun-Yat-Sen, Joyce brings in the latter's provisional capital, Hangchow.

90.34   Meirdreach an Oincuish! *merdrech* (Ir.) = whore; *Oinciu* (Bog Latin) = Ireland

108.29, 109.01   Naysayers ... cant.(?) Bearlagair Na Saer is the vernacular of the Masons (*see also below*)

202.20   gemman's *gemin* (Ir.) = fetter

219.03   scrab *scrab* (BNS) = shilling

.18   fern may cald us. With Finn MacCool *fern* (BNS) = man (?)

223.10   drim and drumming on her back *druim* (Ir.) = back

.28   A darktongues, kunning: followed by anagrams of 'heliotrope'. On p. 12, Macalister describes a gloss to the *Senchus Mor* which tells how two *filé* (poets) argued before Conchobar over who should get a judgeship: ' ... they spoke "in a dark tongue" so that the chieftains standing by were unable to understand them.' Macalister says in a footnote that in the tenth century someone made this into a story, 'The Colloquy of the Two Sages', and in the story the disputants 'confound each other with obscure allusive kennings'.

234.30, ?250.19, .21   liber as they sea *liber* (Bog Latin) = sea

235.16   Oncaill's *onncaill* (Bog Latin) = bury

236.08   Niomon *Nionon* (Bog Latin) = heaven

237.33   Labbeycliath *cliath* (Bog Latin) = cleric

238.35   Teomeo! Daurdour! *Teo* (Bog Latin) = God; *Daur* (Bog Latin) = God

239.31   a place where pigeons carry fire to seethe viands: a BNS sentence (*The Secret Languages*, p. 34) is translated as 'I saw pigeons bringing fire to boil meat at Dublin'

240.12   munchaowl *munchaol* (Bog Latin) = bad

.13   bletchendmacht of the golls *betchennacht* (Bog Latin) = blessing; *goll* (Bog Latin) = blind

241.28   gudth *gudth* (BNS) = whore

242.20   samhar tionnor *samhar* (BNS) = podex; *tionnor* (BNS) = podex

243.29   Alpoleary *Ealp O'Laoghre* (BNS) is riming-slang for Baile Atha Cliath (Dublin); *alp* (BNS) = town

244.07   Ondslosby *Ondslosbu* (Bog Latin) = Britain; (by, Norw. = town)

.14   ruodmark *ruodmarg* (Bog Latin) = bog

.30   Luathan *luathan* (Bog Latin) = bird

246.27   bartrossers *bertroser* (Bog Latin) = brother

.33   Bettlimbraves *betlin* (Bog Latin) = contest

250.34   cac *cac* (Ir.) = excrement

251.04   mun *mun* (Ir.) = urine

255.04   Tamor *tamor* (Bog Latin) = earth

259.01   Till tree from tree, tree among trees, tree over tree become stone to stone, stone between stones, stone under stone for ever—a BNS sentence (*The Secret Languages*, p. 237) is translated as 'Stone to stone, stone between two stones, and stone over stone.' It is a saying which refers to the bonds of Masonry.

277.21   Blath *blath* (Ir.) = flower

290.19, 301.08 Multalusi ... moultylousy *motuillsi* (Bog Latin) = myself (?)

296.06, 296.F1 batom ... Parsee ffrench (with Percy French) *batoma* (Shelta) = policeman; also a Canon J. F. M. ffrench, who collected Shelta words.

323.26   Riland's *Rilantus* (Shelta) = Ireland

338.14   mwilshsuni *mwil*, or *mwilsa* (Shelta) = I, me; *suni* (Shelta) = see

.21   urdlesh. Shelltoss *Sheldru* is one of the names of Shelta; *see* 'Tincurs tammit!', 338.25

.35   minkerstary *Minker's tari* is one of the names of Shelta

339.05   metchennacht *metchennacht* (Bog Latin) = a curse; *see* 'Bog carsse' in the next line

.06   gam cant *Gam Cant* is one of the names of Shelta

346.32   spurk *spurk* (Shelta) = to flirt, with other related meanings, expressing various degrees of immorality

347.01   midril *midril* (Shelta) = devil

Adaline Glasheen

japlatin, with my yuonkle's owlseller (467.14)

‹ ∼∽∼∿∼∿∼∿∼∿∼∿∼∿∼∿∼∿∼∿∼∿∼∿∼∿∼∿∼∿∼ ›

'The Japanese came to see me and was delighted with the japlatin I showed him . . .' (*Letters*, I, p. 242)

31.30	japijap . . . -cherrily . . . tree
36.04	hakusay = Hokusai; *haku* = to wear
54.33	mutsohito. *hito* = person; *muttsu* is a word for 'six' but would never be used with 'person'. (Different numerative system)
70.30	sake
81.33	Mention of the Sino-Japanese War. Vico's theory of history is expressed by reducing the two countries to the common denominator of the all-hero: Japan = Nippo-Napoleon *v* Wellington in Chinese form ('Wei-Ling-Taou')
90.27	yappanoise
96.12	mushymushy: the Japanese use *mushi-mushi* as a form of telephone greeting, equivalent to 'hello'. Used only on the telephone.
200.23	*shoben* = urine
231.09	*Shina* = China; with 231.10: *yoru* = night, *yume* = dream
233.34	*tsuki* = moon; *saki* = tip; *also sukiyaki*
233.35	Makoto *makoto* = truth, reality, sincerity
244.18	Reference to the Japanese manner of speech in which one's interlocutor's property, wife, etc. is referred to with the honorific, but one's own as lowly; *haha* = mum; *cheechee* = dad
244.26	Noh
245.02	Kikikuki *kiku* = to listen, hear, ask
276.15	Nippon
287.F4	Reference to the linguistic theory that Japanese is related to the ugro-altaic languages (Finnish and Hungarian)
312.18	*to* = and
315.22	nogeysokey = *Nagasaki*

317.02	Here, Mr Thornton Wilder points out, St Patrick appears as 'Patriki san', a Japanese. He adds that on page 609 St Patrick is a Japanese. This is so, as he is called a 'Chrystanthemlander' (609.32) and is accompanied by bonzes or oriental priests; 'pompommy' (609.33) reinforces the chrysanthemum reference, while the scene is set by the 'risen sun' (609.20)
320.05	*fuyu* = winter; *fuku* = suit
329.10	bonzai and Nippon
336.20	*shin* = truth; read with 'Drouth is stronger than faction' (same line)
339.02	*sayonara* = farewell; *san* = Mr (Mr Pokehole)
339.03	*ano* = that; *yato* = burglar; ... -dy Icon *daikon* = Japanese turnip
354.24	samuraised = Samurai
408.26	Bonzeye *banzai* = a cheer
484.26-7	Here all the forms of the word 'I', 'myself' are used, plus possibly the verb *oiru* (= to grow old): *watakushi* = I; *watashi* = I, used between friends; *boku* = familiar form of I; *jibun* = myself. The word 'Honorific' at the end of line 27, together with ' ... remembrance to spit [speak] humble ... ' speaks of the Japanese use of the prefix 'O' or honourable before the name of another's property while speaking humbly (without the 'O') of one's own. *See also* 244.18 (of this list).
500.20	Zinzin *zenzen* = nothing
531.35	Yokan: a Japanese confection, especially with horehound (531.25)
535.19	Noksagt = Nagasaki
535.20	shugon = *shogun*
539.11	shintoed = Shinto
542.25	*to* = and, making 'Ladies and Gentlemen'; same usage at 391.21 in 'Romeo and Juliet'
548.09	hochsized = Hokusai
550.28	kiotowing = Kyoto
611.11	noh
612.11	kirikirikiring *kiri* = fog
612.18	shiroskuro: made up from the Japanese words *shiroi* (white) and *kuroi* (black). It is also the word *chiaroscuro* which is made up of two Italian words with substantially the same meaning.
612.20	Iro's *iro* = colour

Philip L. Graham

53

A Passage in Albanian

≈≈≈

On 114.25, we find the word 'Dalbania'. This suggests that its neighbours may have a meaning in Albanian. I do not know the language. (Anybody who does should be able to make both additions and deletions.) However, the words on my list do have a marked resemblance to the text. And, what is equally important, they seem to have a relevance in the context.

	TEXT	ALBANIAN	MEANING
114.23	ftofty	*ftofte*	cold
	od	*ode*	room
.24	karrig	*karrige*	seat
	darka	*darke*	supper
	disheen	*dysh*	in two parts
.25	voos	*voze*	pot or jar
	got	*gote*	drinking-glass
	racky	*raki*	brandy
	portocal	*portogal*	an orange
.26	buk	*buk*	bread
	sofer	*sofer*	dining-table
.27	softball	*safe*	glass-tumbler
		boll	ample
	sucker	*sugar*	favourite
	motru	*motru*	sister
.28	biribiyas	*bir*	son
		bije (pl. of *bir*)	children
	nippies	*nip*	nephew or grandson
	messas	*mes*	a suckling

(Line 24: I have not been able to find an Albanian meaning for 'cheery'. 'Spolatë'—vine shoot—is the nearest that I came to 'spluttered'.)[1]

The approximate sense is 'a cold room— (?) vine-shoots on the seat, a supper—two courses—of dishes from Albania, a glass of brandy, an orange and some bread on the table, you remember the ample tumbler of our favourite, that sister used to tell—or, maybe, the ample tumbler our

[1] *See AWN*, n.s., vol. I, no. 1, February 1964, pp. 3-4.

favourite sister used to tell us—when we were kids, grandchildren and sucklings . . .'

This is not far from what the passage was like before we translated some of the words into Albanian. Mother—*motru*—becomes a sister. Sofa—*sofer*—is a table. In some cases, the meaning is taken care of elsewhere. Sofa is reflected by *karrige*. Where, in one place, we get 'any quantity' of racky, in the other, an ample tumbler. There are other such displacements, but, in the final result, the only important difference is that one room is cold. In the other version, it's warm. Otherwise, the versions are similar. In each, we have a meal. And a significant part of it is liquid.

It is like a two-part song. Each of the voices is doing slightly different notes—and, occasionally, does it at slightly different times.

But they are singing the same song.

Joyce often describes the device that he is using. He may be doing so this time. Take the phrase—line 24—'a darka disheen of voos from Dalbania.'

1. 'A dark dish of booze from Dalbania.' 2. 'A supper—in two parts —of dishes from Dalbania.' But—if 'voos' is 'voice'—he may also be saying that this supper in the text is being done in two parts. *Two voices from Dalbania.*

One more question. Why 'Dalbania'? Why has the D been added? I suspect that, (like several other words: dapple inn, dapple ann), it's a rough amalgam of Dublin.

Thus this confirms that it is a two-part song. One voice is in Dublin. (This voice uses English.) The other voice is in Albania.

Nathan Halper

Artificial Languages

~~~~~~

FW is written in an 'artificial language' and Joyce was obviously interested in his predecessors. There is a list in his hand, *circa* 1938, of forty languages, apparently all used in *FW* (B.M. Add. MS 47488, f.180): this includes Esperanto, Volapük, and Novial. There are a number of words and even sentences in at least two of these languages throughout *FW*, and these mostly ludicrous.

The earliest of these languages was Volapük, invented by Father Schleyer in 1880. The name is derived from *vola*, 'world', and *pük*, 'speech': the vocabulary is based on oddly distorted roots like these. Joyce may have gained nearly all his knowledge of Volapük (Volapucky, 116.31) from the description by Otto Jespersen in *An International Language*, 1928, p. 34:

> ... the stem itself must always begin and end with a consonant. Accordingly *Academy* becomes *kadem*. R is avoided: *fire* is *fil*, and *red led*. As *s* is the sign of the plural, no word may end in *s*: *rose* is made into *lol*. As *ne* is the negative, such a word as *necessity* is clipped of its initial syllable, and becomes *zesüd*. Not even proper names get off scot-free: *Italy* is *Täl*, and *England Nelij* (*j* pronounced *sh*). *Europe* is *Yulop*, and the other continents, which happen in their natural names to begin and end in vowels, must don the same uniform and are made into *Melop*, *Silop*, *Fikop*, and *Talop* respectively.

That partly explains *FW* 34.31: 'Zessid's our kadem, villapleach, vollapluck. Fikup, for flesh nelly, el mundo nov, zole flen!' (Necessity is our school, Africa for England; *flen* is Vol for *friend*, but *el mundo nov*, the new world, is not Vol but something like Esperanto.) 'Talop's' (241.15) may be Vol for *Australia*, as well as Shelta *talop* ('belly'), Plato, and Dr Slop the man-midwife in *Tristram Shandy*. The weird grammar of Vol includes such things as the first personal pronouns *ob*, *obs*, used as suffixes: *löfobs*, 'we love'. Hence perhaps 'when we lofobsed os so ker' (408.19). *See also* 250.10: 'Spoken./So now be hushy, little pukers!' (pukers = speakers). There must be more.

Volapük was succeeded by Esperanto, invented by L. Zamenhof in 1887; it is the only one of these artificial languages to retain a large following today. It is based mainly on international Latin roots, with some English and German, and has simple inflections (*-o* noun, *-a* adj., *-as* verb present tense, etc.). Compounds are built up by prefixes and suffixes, including one which Joyce like many philologists found ludicrous: the excessive use of *mal-* to denote an opposite, e.g. *Malbone*, 'badly' (565.26); cf. 438.02 'malbongusta', 'in bad taste'. Many of Zamenhof's coinings were excellent, but as Joyce read in Jespersen, *An International Language*, p. 38: 'The most curious example is *edzino* "wife," which is taken from the ending of German *kron-prinz-essin* arbitrarily modified; then as *-in-* is the feminine suffix, *edzo* comes to mean husband and *edzighi* to marry.' Hence 39.24: 'his law language (Edzo, Edzo on).'

In the following sentences I have put the literal translation under the Esperanto text, underlining a word only if it is *not* pure Esperanto, or nearly so:

52.14   Spegulo ne halpas al malbellulo,   Mi Kredas   ke vi
         mirror not helps   ugly person, I   believe that you
         estas prava, Via dote   la   vizago rispondas
         are   right, your as-dowry   the face   replies
                            (adv.)
         fraulino
         miss
         (? 'My face is my fortune, sir she says'; *doto* = dowry; the verb
         should be *respondas*)

160.29   Sgunoshooto   estas preter la tapizo malgranda. Lilegas
            ?   is   by   the carpet little.   He reads
         al si   en sia chambro. Kelkefoje funcktas,
         to himself   in his room.   Sometimes works
         kelkefoje srumpas Shultroj. Houdian Kiel   vi fartas,
         sometimes   ?   shoulders.   ?   How do you fare,
         mia nigra sinjoro?
         my   black sir?
         (I cannot find anything like 'Sgunoshooto', though *šuti* is
         'to shoot, pour'. Correct spellings are *tapišo*, *Li legas*, *čambro*,
         funkcias. There does not seem to be a verb *srumpi*, but the
         dictionary has the very Joycean absurdity *štrumpoj*, 'stockings',
         štrumpetoj, 'socks', equalled only by *fartas* in the how-do-you-
         do theme. 'Houdian' seems to be *hodiau*, 'today'.)

565.25   —Li ne dormis?
            He not slept?

—*S!* *Malbone dormas.*
    Badly   sleeps
—*Kia* *li* *krias* *nikte?*
    What he cries nightly?
—*Parolas* *infanetes.* *S!*
    Words babyish

(*Nokto*, 'night'; *-e*, adverbial; *parolo*, 'word'; *infaneto*, 'baby';
but the inflections are not Esperanto.)

There have been several attempts to reform Esperanto, such as Ido
(1907)—'Idos' (465.13)—but they have never caught on. One of the best
is by the great linguist Jespersen, which he called Novial (*Nov* International
Auxiliary Language) and outlined in the book quoted above. Joyce
salutes his work on 351.15: 'noviality'; but Novial is so logical, easy to
read, and free from absurdities that possibly Joyce found nothing to
use in it. The only trouble is that nobody speaks it.

At least one other artificial language is named in *FW*: 'Adamman'
(267.18). There may be more.

                                        M. J. C. Hodgart

Some Lithuanian Words in *FW*

〰〰〰〰〰〰〰〰〰〰〰〰〰〰〰〰〰〰〰〰〰〰〰〰〰〰〰〰〰〰〰〰〰

Lithuanian seems to be a language associated with ALP ('aulne and lithial', 154.04). I should add that I know no Lithuanian, and have not tried to reproduce its complicated systems of accents. I began by looking up obvious words in Lyall's *Guide to the Languages of Europe* (1932, still in print) which I recommend to those who want to begin their investigations of Estonian, Hungarian, etc. in *FW*. Apart from the instances noted below there must be a good deal of Latvian and Lettish in *FW*. It would be appropriate for someone to investigate this since the Newslitter/Newestlatter is specifically called 'Litvian' on 382.13.

The chief concentration of Lithuanian words is probably III.3, 511-12, as announced by 'lithe' (512.12) and 'antelithial' (512.16).

	TEXT	LITHUANIAN	MEANING
511.11	brollies	*brolis*	brother
	sesuos	*sesuo*	sister
.17	perkumiary	*perkunas*	thunder (as in thunder-word, 'Perko-' 23.05)
	pinnigay	*pinigai*	money
.21	blogas	*blogas*	bad
.27	shubladey's	?*šuba*	dress
.30	siderbrass	*sidabras*	silver
.30	sehdass	*žiedas*	ring
512.07	zodisfaction	*žodis*	word
.08	kished	*kišu, kišti*	to stick, stuff
.08	Vulturuvarnar	*varna*	crow, raven
.16-23	(Refers to the forcible conversion of the Lithuanian pagans to Christianity by the Prussian junkers, as brutal as Cromwell's conquest of Ireland. The illiterate savages say the Credo, but instead of the Cross they get English tea, an English king (Semitic M-L-CH) and English coal.)		
.20	Taiptope	*taip*	yes, so
.21-22	('Instead of a cross the Albatross about his neck was hung')		

.22	kavos	*kava*	coffee
	arbatos	*arbata*	tea
	Malkos	*malkos*	fire-wood
.23	Anglys	*anglys*	coal
.25	namas	*namas*	house
.34-35	bridge ... Tiltass	*tiltas*	bridge

There is another group of words on 186-7:

	TEXT	LITHUANIAN	MEANING
186.11	arklast fore	*arklas*	plough
	arklyst	*arklys*	horse
.22	stoties	*stotis, stoties*	station
.31	grazious	*grazus*	beautiful
	oras	*oras*	air, weather

(Shem says 'beautiful weather' to the whores)

187.01	shillto	*šiltas*	warm
	shallto	*šaltas*	cold
	slipny	*silpnas*	weak
	stripny	*stiprus*	strong

(a shilly-shallying slip of a stripling)

.02	allwhite ...	*baltas*	white (Latvian: Balts,
	balltossic		Baltic languages)
.07	caledosian	*Kaledos*	Christmas
.08	Lieutuvisky	*Lietuva*	Lithuania
.22	Tamstar	*Tamsta*	sir, your grace

As is well known, the word for 'river' appears in many languages in I.8 (e.g., 197.18 'follyo', Hungarian *folyo*; 208.23 *joki*, Finnish; 208.24 'fiumy', Italian; *reka*, Slavic; 208.25 'fluve', Latin; 'gawan', Japanese.) Lithuanian and Lettish for river is 'upe': I think this is used in this way on 202.15-16:
'Push up and push vardar and come to uphill headquarters!' Lith.: *vardas*, 'name'; that is, 'Let's have the names of ALP's lovers.'

ADDENDUM

(The following further notes are based on a study of the relevant MS in the Lockwood Memorial Library.)

All the words listed above are confirmed by the Lockwood MS, with the following exceptions: 202.16, 'vardar'; 511.27, 'shubladey's'; 512.08, 'kished'. The following are also listed:

	TEXT	LITHUANIAN	MEANING
93.08	rawdownhams	*raudonas*	red
180.24	bullugs	*bulve* (MS 'bulluchs')	potatoes
186.28	Mergyt	*mergyte*	little girl
.33	Sergo	*sergantis*	sick
187.21	lovom	*lova*	bed
	labaryntos	*labas rytas* (MS 'labaryts')	good morning
247.19	Melained	*melynas*	blue
392.30	Duna	*duona*	bread (?)

A few other words have not yet been identified.

The following do not appear in the MS but deserve consideration:

67.04, etc.	nackt	*naktis*	night
131.04	Diener	*diena*	day
147.24	dieva	*dieva*	God
172.23	Szasas	*šasas*	skin eruption, scurf
173.34	inkstands	*inkstas*	kidney, testicle
185.34	Esuan	*esu*	I am
189.01	wious pish	*pišu, pišti*	to have sexual intercourse
252.04	Dvoinabrathran	*dvynas*	twin
625.27	dumblynass	*dumblynas*	bog

M. J. C. Hodgart

Borrowed Brogues

~~~~~~

As the *Census* and Atherton have shown, Joyce knew some of the works of George Borrow, with whom he must have shared at least an interest in philology and uncommon languages. It seems probable that Joyce, borrowing a word (93.25) or two, made use of a list of Gypsy Words that is appended to my copy of *The Romany Rye*, London, John Murray, 1908.

chabo = child, lad (13.08, 'chabelshoveller'; 'Miry', in the next line might be *miry* = my, mine)

chive = throw, pass a false coin (65.27, 'chivee chivoo')

dook (Slav) = spirit, soul, divining spirit, demon, ghost (Russ. *duch*) (Joyce often spells 'duke' as 'dook'. This may indicate that the person mentioned is to be considered as a ghost: 32.15, 71.19, 127.17, 309.16—cf. 'appearance', 309.15—330.26, 354.19, 371.36, 395.06, 595.22, 595.30)

drab = drug, poison (60.36, 436.26)

Duvel = God (61.02, 178.35, 350.15, 535.15. Extremes meet once again)

dye = mother (327.34, 375.13, 407.36, 506.06, and cf. *also* 'Die eve, little eve, die!' 215.04)

gav = village, town (56.34, 365.31)

gorgio = non-gypsy, stranger, somebody, policeman (3.08, 458.25; another reason for Shaun's being a policeman)

habben = food, victuals (75.11)

juggal = dog (300.31)

juva = young woman (609.25 ff.?)

kek = none (4.02, 590.19)

lovo = coin; *love* (pl.) = money (187.21; *also* 472.19 'nevertoolatetolove box', which renders 'money-box'; cf. *also* acknowledgment of source at 472.22)

lubbeny = harlot (245.13)

mang = beg (338.32)

mer = to die (349.02)

mullo = dead (151.24)

rawnie = lady, wife (437.18, 526.25 'rawkneepudsfrowse', which also contains 'Frau')

rom = husband, gypsy (391.31)

rovel = he weeps (365.23)

sap = snake (511.33, 595.31, etc.?)

sastra = iron (61.20)

scoppelo = ninny (183.01 'scoppialamina', with Joyce's drug, scopolamine; *see Letters*, I, p. 227; cf. *also* 'borrowed', 183.17)

shan = thou art; *shom* = I am. (Nice confirmation that Joyce's 'I' is Shem, while the other chap is Shaun. *See also* 231.03, 483.04, etc.)

shoon = hear, listen (603.04)

shukaro = hammer (339.18, 357.01 'grobsmid . . . shukar')

sove = sleep (561.08, 607.22)

tacho = true (68.34)

tawnie = of; *tawno* = short, little (68.35)

villaminni, (Hung. *villam*) = it lightens (387.19)

wel = come, go (536.25)

wesh, vesh = forest (525.20)

wust = throw (265.27)

yag = fire (296.19, 302.08, 387.10)

yeck = one (68.35)

Could Joyce have known that Borrow was perhaps impotent: 'So lent she him ear to burrow his manhood . . . and borrow his namas?'? (512.23)

Fritz Senn

III Notes

A More Modern Instance

Was there ever heard of such lowdown blackguardism? Positively it woolies one to think over it.

Henry Miller's *Tropic of Cancer*:

"But I will give you a word that will always make you lucky; you must say it every day, over and over, a million times you must say it. It is the best word there is, Endree . . . say it now . . . OOMAHARUMOOMA!"

"OOMARABOO . . . "

"No, Endree . . . like this . . . OOMAHARUMOOMA!"

"OOMAMABOOMBA . . . "

"No, Endree . . . like this . . .

" . . . but what with the murky light, the botchy print, the tattered cover, the jigjagged page, the fumbling fingers, the foxtrotting fleas, the lieabed lice, the scum on his tongue, the drop in his eye, the lump in his throat, the drink in his pottle, the itch in his palm, the wail of his wind, the grief from his breath, the fog of his brainfag, the tic of his conscience, the height of his rage, the gush of his fundament, the fire in his gorge, the tickle of his tail, the rats in his garret, the hullabaloo and the dust in his ears, since it took him a month to steal a march, he was hardset to memorize more than a word a week."[1]

Here is *déjà vu* with a difference. *FW* 180.17-30.

Cancer was first published in 1934, predating *FW* by five years; in any case, there are differences between the two texts not easily explained. *transition*[2] handily predates *Cancer*, but agrees with *FW* rather than *Cancer* in several of the differences. Answers lie at the furthest remove.

[1] Paris: The Obelisk Press (1934), p. 99. All current editions are reset and introduce slight variations. Obelisk (pp. 92-3) has "lie-a-bed." The American edition is New York: Grove Press, Inc. (1961) (pp. 89-90), reset in the softcover "Black Cat" edition (p. 82); it has "fox-trotting," "lie-a-bed," and "hard-set," and the passage is no longer enclosed in quotation marks as in the other editions. The recent British edition is taken by means of photolithography from the American hardcover.

[2] *transition* 7 (October 1927), p. 44.

This Quarter[3] originally published the passage and Roth pirated it shortly thereafter in *Two Worlds*,[4] cleverly calling it part of "A New Unnamed Work" to distinguish it from "Work in Progress." He also—this time inadvertently, no doubt—changed "hardset" to "hardest." Whether Miller would have understood "hardest" to be a mistake is difficult to say. The lone clue suggests *This Quarter* as the more likely source, for *Cancer* has the text precisely as it appeared there, with the exception of an American "z" given "memorise" and two commas introduced to set off "since it took him a month to steal a march." I seize the clue, for the compounding of piracy by plagiarism would be too full of indignity. Miller got his 123 consecutive words and escaped detection for over 28 years. Let us leave it at that, for the last groan is the worst. The trick is on *Cancer*. The delicious fragment stands so obviously apart from the sargasso surrounding.[5]

Jack P. Dalton

[3] *This Quarter*. Milan, 1.2 (Autumn-Winter 1925-26), pp. 114-5. (*see* Slocum-Cahoon, C.67).

[4] *Two Worlds*. New York, 1.4 (June 1926), p. 552. (*see* Slocum-Cahoon, C.65).

[5] A version of this paper entitled "Communiqué from the Joyce Camp" was accepted for publication in the *International Henry Miller Letter*, Nijmegen, Netherlands, but it has not yet appeared.

When lo (whish, O whish!) mesaw mestreamed, as the green to the gred was flew, was flown, through deafths of durkness greengrown deeper I heard a voice, the voce of *S*haun, vote of the Iri*s*h, voise from afar (and cert no purer puer palestrine e'er chanted panangelical mid the clouds of Tu es Petru*s*, not Michaeleen Kelly, not Mara O'Mario, and *s*ure, what more numerose Italicu*ss* ever raw*s*ucked fri*s*h uov in urinal?), a brieze to Yverzone o'er the brozaozaozing *s*ea, from Inchigeela call the way how it *s*uspired (morepork! morepork!) to *s*cented nightlife a*s* softly a*s* the loftly marconimast*s* from Clifden *s*ough open tireless *s*ecret*s* (mauveport! mauveport!) to Nova Sco*t*ia'*s* listing *s*isterwand*s*. Tubetube! (*FW* 407.11-22, italics mine)

In the early days of transatlantic wireless the Marconi Company maintained sister stations in Clifden (Connemara, co. Galway), where the ruins may still be seen, and Nova Scotia (Glace Bay, Cape Breton Island). The antennae employed were said to be upheld by "masts." So much is plain, but there is more. At the beginning of the century Marconi had "turned his attention to the accomplishment of his great ambition, viz. Transatlantic wireless telegraphy . . . . At St John's in Newfoundland he erected a temporary receiving antenna consisting of a wire 400 ft. long upheld by a box kite, and, employing a sensitive coherer and telephone as a receiver, he was able, on December 12, 1901, to hear "S" signals on the Morse code, consisting of three dots, which he had arranged should be sent out from Poldhu [in Cornwall] at stated hours, according to a preconcerted programme, so as to leave no doubt they were electric wave signals sent across the Atlantic and not accidental atmospheric electric disturbances. This result created a great sensation . . . ." In February following, the experiment was repeated on board a ship, the letter "S" being received at a distance of 2099 m. "In the course of this voyage he noticed that the signals were received better during the night than the daytime, legible messages being received on a Morse printer only 700 m. by day but 1500 by night." (The sonorous prose is that of Prof. J. A. Fleming, an associate of Marconi.) This epochal achievement has been remembered in terms of the "S," and at the time Joyce wrote

69

was still fresh in the minds of men. I find the passage remarkable in several respects, but particularly in its complete fusion of manner and matter. That the references to wireless are narrative rather than ornamental is emphasized in the first speech of this "voce of Shaun": "I, the mightif beam maircanny. . . . " (408.16).

It is interesting to note that ten lines of a preceding paragraph (406.36-407.9) are dominated by "R," for Shaun is determined to have his "roysters," to the extent of covering the summer by means of Revolutionary calendar months having "r"s. He is concerned with letters in more ways than one.

Jack P. Dalton

Dilmun

~~~~~~

... was Dilmun when his date was palmy and Mudlin when his nut was cracked ... like fat, like fatlike tallow, of greasefulness, yea of dripping greasefulness; did not say to the old, old, did not say to the scorbutic, scorbutic; he has founded a house, Uru, a house he has founded to which he has assigned its fate ... (136.01-13)

These lines describe certain attributes of HCE. Please compare the following passages in *The Mythology of All Races*, 13 vols. ed. J. A. MacCulloch, vol. V, *Semitic*, by S. H. Langdon, Boston 1931:

In the Tagtug legend of Paradise, [a Sumerian legend] this primeval land of bliss is located in Dilmun, on the eastern shore of the Persian Gulf. (p. 184)

... the tree of life is the date palm, at least in Sumer (p. 187)

... Dilmun was the Sumerian land and garden of Paradise. A long Sumerian poem on Paradise and the loss of eternal life ... presents ... an almost complete parallel to the Hebrew legend of Adam and the Garden of Eden. (p. 194)

Bits of the poem follow:

None said, 'O disease of the eyes, thou art disease of the eyes.'
None said, 'O headache, thou art headache.'
None said to an old woman, 'Thou art an old woman.'
None said to an old man, 'Thou art an old man.'
...
Thou hast founded a city, thou hast founded a city, to which thou hast assigned its fate.
Dilmun the city thou hast founded, thou hast founded a city to which thou hast assigned its fate. (p. 195)
...
It shall be the ninth day in her ninth month, month of the period of woman.
Like fat, like fat, like tallow. (p. 197)

In a note on p. 389 Langdon says 'URU' is the Sumerian ideogram for 'city'.

From this most interesting book on Semitic myth Joyce could also have learned that *sor* is 'rock' in Hebrew (153.23); that *Ze'eb* is 'the wolf' in Hebrew (480.31); that *Arsa* was an Arabian goddess (98.07); that *sedeq* is Semitic 'justice' (25.24); that *kilim* is Aramaic for 'pig' (186.14); and that *Ea*, whose name means 'god of the house of the waters', is present in *Ea*rwicker. It is my opinion that we need a good study of the use of Hebrew in *FW*.

Adaline Glasheen

Instances Perhaps of the Tetragrammaton
in *Finnegans Wake*

~~~~~~

Tetragrammaton (four-letter) is Greek for what the Jews called *Shem Hammephorash* (distinctly excellent name), the incommunicable name of God. The name and its pronunciation are a sacred mystery of the Jewish priesthood, an ancient hiding of God's real name from his enemies. The four consonants are variously written: IHVH, JHVH, JHWH, YHVH, YHWH, that is, I, J, Y are interchangeable, and so are W, V.

I think it impossible that Joyce should not have put the Tetragrammaton into *FW*, and put it often, for Vico tells us that the first word man heard was one of God's names in the angry thunder. There are a great many gods' names in Joyce's own thunder.

Mr Hart (*Concordance*, p. 515) lists a single example of the Tetragrammaton, 'yav hace', and while I do consider 'yav' to refer to Yahweh, this is not a perfect example of the Tetragrammaton. Neither are some of my own examples perfect.

The first place I looked for the Tetragrammaton was 126-39, where Joyce is listing HCE's names and attributes and perhaps I found it, scrambled and in an acrostic: '*h*im *in W*ynn's *H*otel,' (137.05) my italics. Compare 286.10-11: 'Hickey's, hucksler, Wellington's Iron', and note 'HEPTAGRAMMATON' in the right margin.

There may be in *FW* dozens of intended or accidental conjunctions of the consonants of the Tetragrammaton, but I thought Joyce would make more of it than that. A passage at 123.01-02: 'and why spell dear god with a big thick dhee (why, O why, O why?);' made me think that YHWH reduces to 'why'. This was one possible clue to Joyce's use of the Tetragrammaton. Another clue I caught in studying the 100-letter words: Joyce combines the Tetragrammaton with IHS, causes them to melt together, Father and Son consubstantial. These two clues, 'why' and YHWH-IHS led me to the passages discussed below.

At the bottom of p. 261 we find: 'heaventalk, is he? Who is he? Whose is he? Why is he? Howmuch is he? Which is he? When is he? Where is he? How is he?' The initial letters of all these words are the

73

letters of the Tetragrammaton, over and over. The repeated 'is he' contains IHS.

In pursuit of the word 'why' I direct attention to the passage on p. 597 where someone is trying to get at the meaning of the universe. He is answered with what *is*, when he wants to know *why* it is. The questioner persists in asking 'Why?' and finally gets the answer 'Such me.' If the 'Why?' of the passage is a naming of God, we have another level of meaning and the passage can be interpreted in opposite ways, as when (615.16-17) Anna Livia says certain people 'will come to know good', meaning they will turn out badly or they will come to a knowledge of goodness.

On p. 597 the 'Why?' occurs at lines 9, 12, 16, 19, 21, 22, and at lines 12 and 21 the letter preceding 'Why?' is an h: 'far*th. Why?*' and 'throug*h. Why?*', or the whole four letters of the Tetragrammaton.

That Joyce indeed uses his 'Why?' for the Tetragrammaton is made likelier by 'Tom' in line 30, which is Hebrew 'perfection', and by his combining the Tetragrammaton and IHS in lines 35-6:

> say. You have eaden fruit. (IHS)
> Say whuit. (YHW)
> Say whuit. You have (WHY, IHS)
> You have snakked mid a fish. (IHS, ISH, and Christ as fish)
> whish (all the letters of the Tetragrammaton, and IHS).

Adaline Glasheen

The Geometry Problem

Show that the median, hce che ech, interecting at royde angles the parilegs of a given obtuse one biscuts both the arcs that are in curveachord behind. (283.32)

It seems to me that, in the first place, the problem is best read as follows: 'Show that the median, intersecting at right angles the parallel sides (which are also equal in length) of an obtuse triangle, bisects the arcs that meet behind.' I take it for granted that the triangle, as everywhere else in *FW*, is equilateral as well as isosceles.

If the triangle is to be obtuse, it must be spherical. By the words 'interecting at royde angles the parilegs . . .' I think Joyce must mean 'meeting two sides at the apex and making a right angle with each of them'. For this to be possible the triangle must be the limiting case which is the surface of a hemisphere, and of which the three sides are each one third of the circumference of the same great circle. In other words, the perimeter of the triangle is the circumference of a sphere. Each of the angles is then equal to two right angles. The median lies in the circumference of another great circle making right angles with the first. It therefore makes a right angle with each of two sides at the apex and bisects the other at right angles.

'Parilegs' seems to mean, as I have suggested above, that the sides of the triangle are not only equal but also parallel. In our circular triangle there are three pairs of points at which all three sides are parallel: any apex and the centre of the third side.

When interpreted in this way the solution to the problem is, mathematically speaking, trivial—great circles bisect each other. I believe that this is, nevertheless, what Joyce means. For one thing, the circles intersecting at right angles form a structure which is most important in the general spatial organisation of *FW*. (*See* my *Structure and Motif in Finnegans Wake*, London 1962.) And, in any case, this would seem to be the ideal symbolic union of sphere and triangle. The fact that the problem is overdetermined and the solution trivial is no real objection. Redundancy and repetitiveness are inherent qualities of the universe which *FW* depicts.

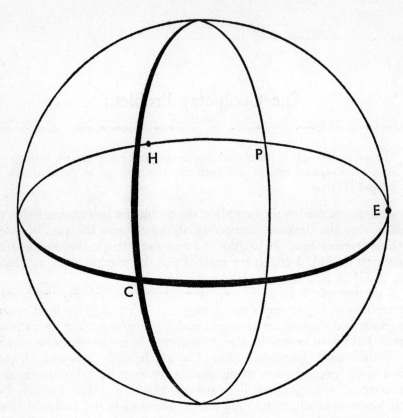

Solution of the geometry problem (283.32). The horizontal great circle is identical with the spherical triangle HCE. The vertical great circle meets the triangle at right angles at points C and P. Point P bisects HE. Sides HE, HC, and EC are parallel at points C and P.

Clive Hart

The Sheep-Tally

Some readers may not be familiar with the English 'sheep-tally'—the modified Welsh cardinal numbers used by shepherds, etc. It exists in many variants. The following version is from Lancashire: Yan, tyan, tethera, methera, pimp, sethera, lethera, hovera, dovera, dick. (*See* 51.16) 'Ya, da, tra, gathery, pimp, shesses, shossafat, okodeboko, nine!'; *and* 457.12; 'yan, tyan, tethera, methera, pimp,'.

Clive Hart

The Crampton Bust

The comment about HCE, beginning at 132.30, derives from the inscription carved below the celebrated bust of Sir Philip Crampton, mentioned in *A Portrait*. (Is it lyric, epic, or dramatic?) The full inscription runs as follows:

> *This fountain has been placed here*
> *A type of health and usefulness*
> *By the friends and admirers*
> *Of Sir Philip Crampton.*
> *It but feebly represents*
> *The sparkle of his genial fancy,*
> *The depth of his calm sagacity,*
> *The clearness of his spotless honour,*
> *The flow of his boundless benevolence.*

Readers who have not visited Dublin in recent years may not know that this extraordinary monument has now been removed to make way for a dull little roundabout.

Clive Hart

A Haka

Ko Niutirenis hauru leish! ... Katu te ihis ihis! Katu te wana wana!
(335.16)

New Zealand and Maori references in the context ('neuziel', 'maor-maoring', 'Wellingthund') indicate that this passage is in Polynesian. The first two lines (335.16 f.) are taken from a well-known and fairly modern *haka*:

Ko Niu Tiireni, e ngunguru nei
               aa-ha-haa ! ! (repeat)
(It is New Zealand, rumbling here!—i.e., making itself heard.)

At line 19 there is a variation on a further snippet from the same *haka*:

Ka tuu te ihiihi ! Ka tuu te wanawana !
(Now is seen the fearfulness, the awfulness.—i.e., of the warriors in their dance.)

The refrain is repeated in lines 4 and 22 of this page.

Clive Hart

(On information received
from Messrs Bruce Biggs and Nathan Halper)

Marginalia from Conversations with Joyce

In 1936 Joyce was on his way back to Paris from Copenhagen. He stopped off in Bonn to talk to Professor Ernst Robert Curtius, whose work in introducing German readers to *Ulysses* he greatly appreciated. 'I want to prove to you' he told him, 'that I am not suffering from softening of the brain'. (Ellmann, p. 709.)

What was said in this conversation was not entirely lost, for Professor Curtius was taking notes on the blank pages of his copy of *Anna Livia Plurabelle* (New York, Crosby Gaige: no. 18 of 800 signed copies). His wife, Ilse Curtius, has kindly permitted these notes to be transcribed. Professor Curtius was completely bilingual (German and French) and made notes in both languages as a matter of course. In addition he was fluent in English: Mrs Curtius reports that the conversations with Joyce, both in Germany and in Switzerland, were always conducted in English. The following notes are left in the language in which they were taken down:

On blank leaf opposite title page:
    music
    calembour
    comical side
    shamrock: pun
On first blank leaf after text:
    Warum verwandeln sich die Weiber in Baum und Stein?
    [This is written in a small neat hand—probably to remind himself to ask Joyce. The 'answer' is written in a larger, more hurried hand—as are all the other notes.]
    bedeuten lebendes (Liebe) und Tod
    de rure albo Motto von Papst Hadrian
On third blank leaf after text:
    4. Teil des 2ten Teils alle gehen nach Hause
    12-4 action takes place in the train
On fifth blank leaf after text:
    Noah hatte 1 Regenbogen—So der alte Viking.

rainbow theme occurs 20 times.

poppy-narancy-giallia-chlora-marinka . . . 7 farben
7 girls. lunar rainbow

Shaun is a great boaster. He teaches the birds to
sing: Do re mi

The night is an absurd thing.
The book is absurd.

On the inside back cover:

fox & gripes ⎫
⎬ mookes
lion & mouse ⎭

————

decorative scheme
I have no convictions of any kind.
1st 8 episodes are a kind of immense shadow

kl. familie im Geburtsort der Isolde. Kinder spielen
die Weltgeschichte.

Schlafzimmer der Kinder über der Bar, wo der Vater
Bauern betrunken macht.

When their studies are finished, the children are
put to bed.

The nature of these notes clearly supports the supposition that they are
taken from conversation with Joyce. I have left the punctuation, or lack
of it, unchanged. *Newslitter* readers will be able to follow up hints from
these notes on their own. (To mention only one: the generation of
'mookes' from the tale of the lion and mouse as well as the fox and
grapes—this is supported by Joyce's postcard to H. S. Weaver of 16
April 1927, 'the mouse and the grapes'). The reference to the seven girls
of the *lunar* rainbow is *FW* 102.25.

Breon Mitchell

The Four Absolutes

~~~~~~

With hapsalap troth, hipsalewd prudity, hopesalot honnessy, hoopsaloop luck. (325.08)

This is a reference to the imperatives of the Oxford Group (Buchmanites): Absolute truth, absolute purity, absolute honesty, absolute love. The group had its inception in the early twenties, and I believe that it received much support from rich residents of Switzerland, many of whom were Americans. There seem to be allusions to Cognac and to shame in 'honnessy', and to ring-tossing at fairs for a prize in 'hoopsaloop luck', but the cream of the lot is, I think, 'hipsalewd prudity'. The groups were always criticized harshly because they purged themselves by confession to mixed groups of young people—with considerable emphasis on the sins of the flesh. The process was obviously titillating to prurience (and, in Joyce's view, to abstain from heterosexual expression was prudish). All of Joyce's absolutes suggest sex: lap, hip, salot (hinting at French *salaud*), hoop, etc.

Ruth von Phul

PUBLICATIONS OF THE
AUSTRALIAN HUMANITIES RESEARCH COUNCIL

ANNUAL REPORTS

1 1956-7. 75c.
2 1957-8, containing A. D. Trendall: *The Felton Greek Vases in the National Gallery of Victoria* (out of print)
3 1958-9, containing A. Grenfell Price: *Western Influences in the Pacific and its Continents* (out of print)
4 1959-60, containing John Anderson: *Classicism*. 75c.
5 1960-1, containing A. G. Mitchell: *The Australian Accent*. 75c.
6 1961-2. 75c.
7 1962-3, containing A. Boyce Gibson: *Works of Literature and Work in Philosophy*. 75c.
8 1963-4, containing J. J. Auchmuty, *Problems of Nineteenth Century Biography: Wyse —Acton—Lecky*; and C. P. FitzGerald, *Biographical Essay on Oriental Studies in Australia since 1958*. 75c.
9 1964-5, containing G. P. Shipp: *Greek Culture in Perspective*; and R. R. Dyer, *Bibliographical Essay on Classical Studies in Australia since 1958*. 75c.
10 1965-6, containing W. K. Hancock: *Ordeal by Thesis*; and K. V. Sinclair, *Bibliographical Essay on Medieval Studies in Australia since 1958*. 75c.
11 1966-7, containing R. M. Crawford: *'Per Quale Iddìo': Machiavelli's Second Thoughts*. $1.00.

MONOGRAPHS

1 *The Hopetoun Blunder*, J. A. La Nauze, 1958. 50c.
2 *Mallarmé's 'L'Après-midi d'un Faune'*, A. R. Chisholm, 1958. 50c.
3 *Form and Meaning in Valéry's 'Le Cimetière marin'*, James R. Lawler, 1959. 50c.
4 *The Art of E. M. Forster*, H. J. Oliver, 1960. $1.25.
5 *Bandello and the 'Heptameron'*, K. H. Hartley, 1960. 75c.
6 *Walter Pater*, R. V. Johnson, 1961. 75c.
7 *The Melbourne Livy*, K. V. Sinclair, 1961. $1.25.
8 *Essays in Mycenaean and Homeric Greek*, G. P. Shipp, 1961. $1.50.
9 *The Thesis of 'Paradise Lost'*, G. A. Wilkes, 1961 (out of print)
10 *The Similes of the 'Iliad' and the 'Odyssey' Compared*, D. J. N. Lee, 1964. $1.50.
11 *'Double Profit' in 'Macbeth'*, H. L. Rogers, 1965. $1.25.
12 *The 'Enragés': Socialists of the French Revolution?* R. B. Rose, 1965. $2.00.

OCCASIONAL PAPERS

1 *The Birth of Modern Comedy of Manners*, T. B. L. Webster, 1959. 20c.
2 *Notes on the 'Dyskolos' of Menander*, J. H. Quincey, W. Ritchie, G. P. Shipp, and A. P. Treweek, 1959. 20c.
3 *Aspects of Philhellenism in Antiquity*, Sir Frank Adcock, 1961. 20c.
4 *The End of Roman Imperialism*, E. T. Salmon, 1961. 20c.
5 *Research in Australia and Contacts with Europe*, A. Cambitoglou, 1964. 20c.
6 *The Berlin Painter*, Sir John Beazley, 1964. $1.00.
7 *Robert Frost and his Reputation*, D. Grant, 1965. 20c.
8 *The Future of the Humanities in the Australian Universities*, J. McManners and R. M. Crawford, 1965. 20c.
9 *The Neurotic in Literature*, Mario Praz, 1965. 20c.
10 *The Rationalization of Library Resources in Australia*, N. Stockdale and J. J. Graneek, 1967. 60c.
11 *Postgraduate Studies in the Humanities in Australia: Three Essays*, W. K. Hancock, P. H. Partridge, and R. W. V. Elliott, 1967. $1.50.
12 *The Brygos Painter*, A. Cambitoglou, 1968. $2.00.

E

The Felton Greek Vases in the National Gallery of Victoria, A. D. Trendall, 1958. $1.20.
The Humanities in Australia—A Survey with Special Reference to the Universities, ed.
A. Grenfell Price. Angus & Robertson, 1959, $4.20.
Classicism, John Anderson, 1960. 20c.
The Australian Accent, A. G. Mitchell, 1961. 20c.
Works of Literature and Work in Philosophy, A. Boyce Gibson, 1963. 20c.
Problems of Nineteenth Century Biography: Wyse—Acton—Lecky, J. J. Auchmuty,
1964. 20c.
Ordeal by Thesis, W. K. Hancock, 1966. 20c.
Bibliographical Essay on Medieval Studies in Australia since 1958, K. V. Sinclair, 1966. 50c.
'Per Quale Iddìo': Machiavelli's Second Thoughts, R. M. Crawford, 1967. 75c.
A Wake Digest, Clive Hart and Fritz Senn (eds), 1968. $2.00.

AHRC publications are obtainable from booksellers